Federal Sentencing Guidelines: A Guide for Internal Auditors

by
Paul E. Fiorelli, JD, MBA
and Cynthia J. Rooney, PhD, CPA

The Institute of Internal Auditors
Research Foundation

Disclosure

ISBN 0-89413-361-6
96377 5/96
First Printing

SUCCESS BEGINS WITH A STRONG FOUNDATION

At The Institute of Internal Auditors Research Foundation, we believe *Success Begins with a Strong Foundation*. We want to help you to be successful by providing valuable research reports that enable you to remain knowledgeable in all aspects of internal auditing.

Our goal is to help you to meet *your* goals. We want you to know that we are here for you, always providing that *Strong Foundation* you need. Our valuable, ground-breaking research is presented in concise, insightful reports to help you to stay informed, competitive, and ready to meet the challenges you face in the workplace every day.

Count on us to provide a *Strong Foundation* for your continued professional success.

THE INSTITUTE OF INTERNAL AUDITORS RESEARCH FOUNDATION
249 Maitland Avenue
Altamonte Springs, FL 32701-4201
407 830-7600, Ext. 276
FAX 407 831-5171

2/96312 bd/bd
Printed in the U.S.A.

Please Share Your Views With Us.

We value your opinion. Please use the area below to provide any comments you have on this publication:

Name of publication: ______________________

Comments: ______________________

____

____

Do you have comments regarding any other Foundation publications?

Name(s) of publication(s): ______________________

____

____

Comments: ______________________

____

____

Do you have any suggestions for future research topics?

____

____

____

Please mail to: The Institute of Internal Auditors Research Foundation
249 Maitland Avenue, Altamonte Springs, FL 32701-4201

COMMENTS

Become a Part of The Foundation.

☐ I am returning this card with my pledge in the amount of U.S. $ ____________.

☐ My check is made payable to The IIA Research Foundation in the amount of U.S. $____________.

☐ Charge my ☐VISA ☐MasterCard ☐American Express in the amount of U.S. $____________.

Acct. # ______________________ Exp. Date ________

Signature ______________________
(Signature required for pledge or charge card)

Name: ______________________

IIA Member? ☐ Yes Member # ____________ ☐ No

Title: ______________________

Organization: ______________________

Organization Address: ______________________

City: ____________ State/Province: ____________

Country: ____________ ZIP/Mail Code: ____________

Phone: ____________ FAX: ____________

☐ My organization has a Matching Gift Program. Please contact:

____
Name Phone No.

INS 96

Thank you for supporting The IIA Research Foundation, your Strong Foundation for Success in internal auditing.

Please mail to: The Institute of Internal Auditors Research Foundation
Attn: Walter Liss, 249 Maitland Avenue, Altamonte Springs, FL 32701-4201

CONTRIBUTION

CONTENTS

List of Tables and Figures

ABOUT THE AUTHORS

Paul E. Fiorelli, JD, MBA, is a Professor of Legal Studies at Xavier University. He has written several articles dealing with the Federal Sentencing Guidelines and is a frequent speaker on the topic. Fiorelli teaches the Law and Ethics courses within Xavier's undergraduate and graduate business programs, and consults in the area of business ethics. He also has accounting experience as a tax attorney with Ernst & Whinney.

Cynthia J. Rooney, PhD, CPA, is an Assistant Professor of Accounting and Information Systems at Xavier University. Her published works include articles dealing with the Federal Sentencing Guidelines, accounting education, and other audit and accounting issues. Rooney teaches auditing and financial accounting within Xavier's undergraduate and graduate business program. She has accounting experience as an auditor with Ernst & Whinney.

DEDICATION

We would like to dedicate this book to our families:
Liz, Katherine, Stephanie, and Joseph
and
Brian, Kate, and Allison

ACKNOWLEDGMENTS

We appreciate the support of The Institute of Internal Auditors Research Foundation. We express special gratitude to Thomas Warga, CIA, Senior Vice President and General Auditor for New York Life Insurance Company, for his support, encouragement, and guidance throughout this project. We would also like to thank the project management team and the staff of The IIA for their assistance in completing this project. Thanks also to the numerous individuals who participated in interviews and the respondents to our survey who provided valuable insight and perspective. Special thanks to Mr. William Giffin of Sears for his help in obtaining Sears' Code of Business Conduct.

Project Management Team
Thomas Warga, CIA, *Project Manager*
David S. Kowalczyk, CIA
Claire Beth Nilsen
Donald F. Ricketts
Kathryn A. Schooley, CPA

The Institute of Internal Auditors
Headquarters Staff
William G. Bishop III, CIA —
President, The IIA; Executive Director,
The IIA Research Foundation
Basil H. Pflumm, CIA, *Director of Research*
Walter E. Liss, *Director of Finance*
James H. Thompson, CIA, *Manager of Research*
Sue DiBlanda, *Research Administrator*
Elizabeth Bossarte, *Research Coordinator*
Lee Ann Campbell, *Publications Editor*

EXECUTIVE SUMMARY

The Federal Sentencing Guidelines for Organizations, passed in 1991, provide incentives for corporations to maintain adequate compliance programs. Organizations found guilty of a wide range of federal law violations can reduce their fines by demonstrating due diligence in establishing an effective compliance program. The Guidelines include seven minimum requirements for a compliance program: (1) establish adequate compliance standards and procedures to reduce the prospect of criminal conduct; (2) assign high-level personnel to oversee the compliance program; (3) use due care not to delegate responsibility to a person with a "propensity to engage in illegal activities;" (4) communicate compliance procedures through publications and training; (5) audit the program and maintain a violation reporting system; (6) consistent enforcement of the compliance program; and (7) make a reasonable response to an offense and modify the program to prevent future offenses. Implementing, maintaining, and evaluating an effective compliance program requires significant effort. Because of the independent appraisal service already provided by the internal auditing function, many organizations are looking to internal auditors to take the lead in assuring that the organization has an acceptable compliance program.

This study investigates the impact of the Federal Sentencing Guidelines on internal auditors. The study was conducted by reviewing the literature, interviewing numerous internal audit directors and compliance officers, and obtaining survey responses from internal auditors and compliance officers nationwide. Results indicate that the majority of the respondents were familiar with the Guidelines, but were not always convinced that the Guidelines would have a significant impact on their organizations. Sometimes this was due to existing industry requirements; other explanations suggest that respondents were not convinced that the Guidelines could apply to them. Respondents to the survey also indicated that key individuals from internal audit often served in oversight roles as members of the compliance committee. Numerous respondents indicated that internal audit was responsible for "auditing" the compliance program. All respondents rated their organization regarding compliance with the seven requirements of the Guidelines listed above. The mean responses on the seven items varied between 3.32 and 3.86 using a 5-point scale (1 = Very Low, 5 = Very High). Frequency distributions of the ratings are presented in related chapters. Regarding the type of involvement internal auditors have with each of the seven requirements, most indicated frequent involvement with investigating reported failures, and many indicated involvement with design and monitoring activities.

This report begins with an introduction in Chapter 1, followed by an overview of the Federal Sentencing Guidelines in Chapter 2. Chapter 3 explains the relationship between the COSO report on Internal Controls and the Guidelines. Chapter 4 provides a summary of the research methodology. Chapters 5 through 11 analyze the "seven minimum requirements" of a compliance program. Each chapter includes: (1) an overview of the requirement, (2) a summary of survey results, (3) the role of internal auditors, and (4) business considerations in meeting the requirement. Chapter 12 discusses the issues of voluntary disclosure, privilege, and the possibility that internal investigations may be used against the organization in subsequent litigation, and Chapter 13 offers concluding remarks.

CHAPTER 1
INTRODUCTION

Internal auditors are charged with evaluating the effectiveness of various programs, including compliance programs. One problem with evaluating compliance programs is the lack of benchmarks against which auditors can measure their own programs. The Federal Sentencing Guidelines (Guidelines) provide benchmarks by defining the seven minimum requirements of an effective program to prevent and detect violations. Due to the potential financial impact of noncompliance, internal auditors should take a leadership role in understanding and operationalizing the requirements of the Guidelines.

Based upon a recent survey, many internal auditors are not convinced that the Guidelines have much impact on their organizations. Some believe that the Guidelines must be unimportant since no major "headline" cases have been reported. The lack of cases is due to the Department of Justice's decision not to prosecute cases under the Guidelines for violations that occurred before November 1, 1991. Since cases involving large organizations are complex and take years to develop, auditors should not confuse a lack of activity with a lack of importance.

One case that has received attention involves Daiwa Bank, whose officials pleaded guilty to covering up more than $1 billion in trading losses. While the potential fine could have been $1.3 billion under the Federal Sentencing Guidelines, prosecutors gave Daiwa significant credit for cooperating, and agreed to a $340 million criminal fine on February 29, 1996. Daiwa received this consideration because of the guilty plea and repaid $377 million that one of its employees had taken from custody accounts. The Daiwa case underscores the importance of understanding the Guidelines.

The Role of Internal Auditing

Internal auditors have definite responsibilities to their organizations regarding the Guidelines and the need for compliance systems. Section 300 of the *Standards for the Professional Practice of Internal Auditing (Standards)* states that "The scope of internal auditing should encompass the examination and evaluation of the adequacy and effectiveness of the organization's system of internal control and the quality of performance in carrying out assigned responsibilities." This focus on internal control encompasses the same controls required in an effective compliance program per the Guidelines. In addition, Section 320 states that "Internal auditors should review the systems established to ensure compliance with those policies, plans, procedures, laws, and regulations which could have a significant impact on operations and reports, and should determine whether the organization is in compliance." This section seems to require internal auditors to evaluate the organization's compliance with the Guidelines, since noncompliance could have a significant impact on operations. Section 320.01 places the burden of establishing compliance programs on management, and the internal auditor is given the responsibility of "determining whether the systems are adequate and effective." In dealing with compliance programs, internal auditors, regardless of their involvement in the design of the program, are responsible for "auditing" its effectiveness. The *Standards* strongly suggests that internal auditors carefully evaluate their organizations' compliance with the Federal Sentencing Guidelines.

Benefits of Compliance with the Guidelines

Several important benefits result from understanding and complying with the Guidelines. These advantages include: (1) fine minimization, (2) avoiding criminal prosecution, (3) improved settlement negotiations with the government, and (4) better employee morale.

Fine Minimization

For an example of fine reductions, consider two similar organizations that have each been fined $20,000,000. "Goodco" had an effective program to prevent and detect violations, but had a few problem employees who were responsible for the infraction. Once detected, Goodco conducted an investigation, self-reported, and cooperated with the governmental proceedings. Ultimately, it accepted responsibility and revised its procedures to minimize similar risks in the future. "Badco's" top management suspected that problems were present, but sent implicit messages that the improper behavior would be tolerated as long as the short-term goals were met. They "stonewalled" every government investigation and denied responsibility, even after they were convicted.

Under the 1991 Federal Sentencing Guidelines, Goodco and Badco would receive significantly different treatment. Federal judges sentencing Goodco would reduce its $20,000,000 fine by up to 95 percent, resulting in a $1,000,000 sanction, because Goodco followed the "4 C's" — Comply, Contact, Cooperate, and be Contrite. Alternatively, Badco's $20,000,000 fine could be increased fourfold to $80,000,000. The carrot and stick approach to sentencing means that organizations can control this 80:1 swing in fines by following the Guidelines.

Of the "4 C's," internal auditors have the most direct interaction with "compliance." Chapters 5 through 11 describe what constitutes an effective compliance program as defined by the Guidelines. Internal auditors should also be familiar with the remaining three "C's" in order to be a part of the decision about the advisability of contacting, cooperating, and contrition.

The Guidelines explain how organizations that voluntarily disclose violations to the appropriate authorities, cooperate in the investigation, and accept responsibility can qualify for significant fine reductions. A "contacting" organization will self-report possible wrongdoings after conducting a thorough review. Corporations will not qualify for this aspect of fine reductions if their government contact is perceived to be a last-minute response to an imminent investigation by the authorities. To receive this smaller fine, any government reporting must also come from the organization itself and not from a "whistleblower."

The Guidelines also allow fine reductions for organizations that fully cooperate and accept responsibility, regardless of their voluntary disclosure. "Cooperative" organizations work with the authorities once the government has begun its investigations. Reductions are even available if an organization only accepts responsibility ("contrition") for its wrongdoings, without cooperating in the investigation. Accepting responsibility typically means entering a guilty plea and not putting the government to its burden of proof at trial. It may also include having company CEOs stand before the sentencing judge and express remorse for their organizations' actions.

Criminal Prosecution

The Guidelines have given prosecutors broad discretionary power in determining whether to charge potential violators. One factor that prosecutors will analyze in deciding whether to criminally charge an organization is the adequacy of the organization's compliance programs. If the organization has: (1) an effective compliance program, (2) infractions committed by lower-level employees, and (3) modifications to its systems to avoid repeat offenses, it may convince the prosecutor that no substantial justification exists to bring a criminal charge against the defendant. Organizations that make a persuasive case may avoid the inconvenience and expense associated with a criminal investigation and trial.

Settlements

In addition to monetary fines, the government may impose a rigid compliance program on a violator as a term of probation. While there have not been many examples of government negotiated compliance programs, the Corporate Integrity Program imposed upon National Medical Enterprises (NME) offers a glimpse into one costly and intrusive system.

NME managed different health care activities. In 1993 federal investigators accused the company of billing fraud, improper payments to induce referrals, and improper waivers of copayments and deductibles. NME's settlement agreement with the government included: (1) contracting with an outside accountant to audit its billing practices and report any material violations to the Department of Health and Human Services, (2) contracting with an outside medical association about the length of stay of patients within its psychiatric facilities, (3) reporting to the Department of Health and Human Services about the payment to physicians, and only allowing payments after being approved by outside counsel, (4) adopting standards of conduct which would be circulated to all employees, and (5) training all employees on their new policies and procedures. These additional, cumbersome practices may have been avoided by a proactive compliance program.

Employee Morale

Compliance programs that satisfy the Guidelines can have the added benefit of improved employee morale. Working in an environment of trust has a strong positive impact, which will become more apparent in the following chapters. Methods that organizations can use to create a trusting environment include: (1) encouraging employees to report wrongdoings without fear of retaliation, (2) disciplining consistently for similar violations, and (3) providing additional reporting mechanisms (i.e., hotlines) to express concerns. These are all components of an effective program to prevent and detect violations which will also create an environment of trust that enhances employee attitudes.

Impact on Organizations

Some internal auditors believe that the Guidelines only apply to large defense contractors. This misguided belief could prove costly to their organizations. The United States Sentencing Commission (Commission) conducted a survey of organizations sentenced pursuant to the Guidelines from November 1, 1987, to June 30, 1995, and the results demonstrate its applicability to a wide range of organizations. Regarding size, the survey indicated that: (1) 56% of the offenders had less than 20 employees, (2) 23% had 20 to 99 employees, (3) 16% had 100 to 499 employees, and (4) 5% had 500 or more employees. The survey also showed that organizations were sentenced for violations which would affect defense contractors and non-defense contractors alike. The survey percent and corresponding violations were: (1) 32% for antitrust, (2) 30% for fraud, (3) 11% for environmental/waste charge violations, (4) 9% for tax, (5) 5% for money laundering, (6) 3% for food & drugs, and (7) 10% for other violations which could include copyright/trademark infringement, export violations, and RICO.

Research Method

To investigate the impact of the Federal Sentencing Guidelines on internal auditors, several methods were employed to collect relevant information. These included a review of the related literature, interviews with leaders of internal auditing departments, interviews with directors of compliance programs, and a nationwide survey of internal auditors and compliance officers.

Review of the Literature

The key literature includes material from the United States Sentencing Commission, published materials on the Guidelines and effective compliance programs, and publications related to internal auditing. Each year the Commission publishes an *Annual Report,* which includes a summary of the offenses and related characteristics of the organizations sentenced under the Guidelines. There are various publishers who provide an abundance of information related to the Guidelines. The Bibliography includes additional reference material such as: (1) *Compliance Programs and the Corporate Sentencing Guidelines* (Kaplan, Murphy, and Swenson, 1995), (2) *Corporate Sentencing Guidelines: Compliance and Litigation* (Rakoff, Blumkin, and Sauber, 1994), (3) the *Annual Report to the Public of the Defense Industry* and, (4) the report on *Corporate Ethics: A Prime Business Asset* (1988).

Interviews with Internal Auditors and Directors of Compliance Programs

In-depth, half-day, personal interviews were conducted with individuals representing seven organizations. The selected organizations represented various industries, including financial institutions, insurance, utilities, consumer products, and defense contractors. In most of the organizations, interviews were conducted with the persons responsible for: (1) the internal auditing department, and (2) the compliance program. If the organization did not have a formal compliance program, only the director of internal auditing was interviewed. In one case, only the ethics officer, who is considered a leader regarding compliance programs, was interviewed. The interviews proved very useful in identifying key issues, concerns, and best practices.

Survey of Internal Auditors and Compliance Officers

To obtain information from a broad group of individuals, a survey was conducted with the assistance of The Institute of Internal Auditors Research Foundation. Questionnaires were mailed to individuals who were identified in The Institute of Internal Auditors' (IIA) database as the highest level internal auditors for their organization. (See Appendix A.) This group represented 469 individuals at the time of the survey, and questionnaires were mailed to the entire group. Individuals receiving a survey were also asked to pass an additional questionnaire along to the compliance officer, or appropriate individual, in their organization. (See Appendix A.) Since not all organizations have compliance programs and because of the potential problems with forwarding an additional questionnaire, the number of compliance officers receiving a survey instrument was expected to be less than the number of internal auditors. From those surveyed, responses were received from 129 internal auditors and 62 compliance officers.

CHAPTER 2
HISTORICAL DEVELOPMENT

Individual Sentencing Guidelines

In 1984 Congress enacted the Comprehensive Crime Control Act. Included within this legislation was a plan to drastically reform existing federal sentencing practices. One of Congress' major complaints was the lack of uniformity in sentencing. While some federal judges were giving convicted offenders probation, others were imposing maximum prison terms under similar circumstances. Congress feared that this lack of uniformity bred contempt and was not an effective deterrent. To remedy this situation, Congress created the United States Sentencing Commission (Commission), composed of seven voting members and one ex-officio member.

Congress instructed the Commission to create sentencing guidelines that all federal judges would follow. The Commission first dealt with individual defendants, and in May 1987 presented Congress with Chapters 1 through 7 of the Federal Sentencing Guidelines Manual. These became law on November 1, 1987. The formula for consistent sentencing under the individual sentencing guidelines analyzed both the severity of the offense and the criminal history of the defendant.

Organizational Sentencing Guidelines

In 1988 the Commission began developing guidelines to deal with organizational crimes. On May 1, 1991, the Commission sent the proposed amendments for sentencing corporate defendants to Congress. Since the proposed amendments were unchallenged, they became effective on November 1, 1991, and were incorporated into the Guidelines Manual as Chapter 8.

Goals

The stated goals of the Sentencing Commission's amendments are to, "provide just punishment, adequate deterrence, and incentives for organizations to maintain internal mechanisms for preventing, detecting and reporting criminal conduct." The Guidelines try to accomplish these goals by: (1) providing victim restitution, (2) divesting crime infested organizations of their assets, and (3) determining an appropriate, additional fine based on the seriousness of the offense and the culpability of the organization.

Fine Calculations

The seriousness of the offense is determined by establishing a base fine, which is the greatest of: (1) the pecuniary loss suffered by the victim, (2) the pecuniary gain received by the defendant, or (3) a penalty determined by analyzing the Offense Level Fine Table. (See Table 2-1). These table amounts are calculated by using the base offense level, with any adjustments, as established in the Guidelines Manual. The fine range from Table 2-1, before any multiplier or reducer is applied, is $5,000 to $72,500,000. With minimum and maximum multipliers of 5% to 400%, the Table 2-1 range is effectively extended from $250 ($5,000 * 0.05) to $290,000,000 ($72,500,000 * 4.0).

Culpability Score

Regardless of whether the base fine is calculated by the greater of the pecuniary gain by the defendant, loss by the victim, or from the offense level table, this amount can be either increased or decreased, based on an organization's culpability score. For any given culpability score, the judge has the discretion of imposing a fine within a minimum and maximum range. (See Table 2-2). A higher culpability score establishes a higher minimum and maximum range of multipliers. The maximum multiplier is four, which has the mathematical effect of multiplying a fine by 400%. A lower culpability score decreases the minimum and maximum multipliers, which can dramatically reduce a fine. The minimum multiplier is 0.05 of

Table 2-1
Offense-Level Fine Table

OFFENSE LEVEL	AMOUNT
6 or less	$ 5,000
7	7,500
8	10,000
9	15,000
10	20,000
11	30,000
12	40,000
13	60,000
14	85,000
15	125,000
16	175,000
17	250,000
18	350,000
19	500,000
20	650,000
21	910,000
22	1,200,000
23	1,600,000
24	2,100,000
25	2,800,000
26	3,700,000
27	4,800,000
28	6,300,000
29	8,100,000
30	10,500,000
31	13,500,000
32	17,500,000
33	22,000,000
34	28,500,000
35	36,000,000
36	45,500,000
37	57,500,000
38 or more	72,500,000

Table 2-2
Minimum and Maximum Fine Multipliers

CULPABILITY SCORE	MINIMUM MULTIPLIER	MAXIMUM MULTIPLIER
10 or more	2.00	4.00
9	1.80	3.60
8	1.60	3.20
7	1.40	2.80
6	1.20	2.40
5	1.00	2.00
4	0.80	1.60
3	0.60	1.20
2	0.40	0.80
1	0.20	0.40
0 or less	0.05	0.20

the fine, which has the mathematical effect of dividing the fine by 20.

The culpability score starts with five points, and may be either increased or decreased depending upon certain factors. As discussed in Chapter 1, fines will be decreased by following the "4 C's" — Comply, Contact, Cooperate, and be Contrite. Effective compliance programs which prevent and detect violations qualify for a three-point reduction from the culpability score. Organizations that self-disclose (contacting), cooperate, and accept responsibility (contrition) qualify for up to a five-point reduction. Those that cooperate with an investigation and accept responsibility (contrition) afterwards can receive a two-point reduction. Finally, organizations that merely demonstrate remorse (contrition) can receive a one point reduction from the score.

Factors That Increase Fines

The culpability score, and thus the fine, will be increased based upon: (1) the size of the organization, (2) involvement of top officials, (3) prior violations, and (4) obstruction of justice.

Size of the Organization

If the organization, or a unit of the organization, had 5,000 or more employees and an individual within high-level personnel either: (1) participated in, (2) condoned, or (3) was willfully ignorant of the offense, add five points to the base score of five points for an aggregate 10 points. The penalty will decrease with the decreasing size of the organization. The respective decrease is: (1) four points for an organization or unit with more than 1,000 employees, (2) three points for an organization with more than 200 employees, (3) two points for an organization with more than 50 employees, and (4) one point for an organization with more than 10 employees.

Involvement of Top Management

The Commission's rationale for increasing the penalty with an organization's increased size is that as a company gets larger, its management becomes increasingly professional. The Commission also believes that when upper-level managers of large corporations tolerate illegal actions, they are abusing their position and breaching the trust placed in them. Also, if the tolerance is pervasive, there is an increased risk of other offenses within the organization.

Prior History
Prior criminal activity of similar offenses will increase the culpability score of organizations. The score will increase by either one or two points depending on how long ago the similar violation occurred. Add two points if the organization committed a second similar offense within the preceding five years. Add one point if the second similar violation occurred within 10 years.

Violation of an Order and Obstruction of Justice
The last two factors to consider in adding to a culpability score deal with: (1) violations of orders, and (2) obstruction of justice. If committing the instant offense violated a condition of probation, add one point to the culpability score. If the organization either obstructed, encouraged, aided, or willfully failed to prevent the obstruction of justice, add three points.

Conclusion

The Organizational Sentencing Guidelines (OSG) have been in existence since November 1, 1991, and cases like Daiwa Bank and NME (both discussed in Chapter 1) reaffirm the potential impact the guidelines can have on any organization. Prosecutors have now had adequate lead time to develop additional criminal cases, and internal auditors should expect more government investigations in the future.

CHAPTER 3
THE RELATIONSHIP OF THE GUIDELINES TO COSO

"Internal Control — Integrated Framework," the 1992 report prepared by the Committee of Sponsoring Organizations (COSO), provided a broad definition of internal control and a framework for evaluating and improving control systems. The COSO report provides the following definition of internal control:

> *Internal control is broadly defined as a process, effected by an entity's board of directors, management, and other personnel, designed to provide reasonable assurance regarding the achievement of objectives in the following categories:*
> - *Effectiveness and efficiency of operations.*
> - *Reliability of financial reporting.*
> - *Compliance with applicable laws and regulations.*
>
> *(COSO, Executive Summary, 1992, p. 1)*

COSO considers these three categories as overlapping, yet distinct. The effectiveness of an internal control system is measured by the ability of the system to provide reasonable assurance to the board of directors and management that these three objectives have been met. In addition to these goals, COSO identified five interrelated components of internal control: (1) control environment, (2) risk assessment, (3) control activities, (4) information and communication, and (5) monitoring. These components combine to form an integrated system of controls. They will be used as the framework to demonstrate the similarities between COSO and the Guidelines.

Guidelines Requirements for an Effective Compliance Program

The Guidelines state that the "minimum requirements" for an effective compliance program are: (1) having compliance standards and procedures that can reduce criminal conduct (FSG#1), (2) specifically designating high-level individuals within the organization to oversee the program (FSG#2), (3) exercising due care not to delegate significant authority to a person known to have criminal tendencies (FSG#3), (4) developing a method of communicating the policies and procedures to all employees and other agents (FSG#4), (5) utilizing internal controls to monitor and audit its systems, and having an additional reporting mechanism where employees can report criminal conduct without fear of retaliation (FSG#5), (6) consistently enforcing the standards through appropriate disciplinary mechanisms (FSG#6), and (7) taking the necessary steps to prevent any similar occurrences in the future, including modifying the compliance program (FSG#7).

COSO and the Guidelines both focus on developing a strong control system. COSO is much broader than the Guidelines, but all of the Guidelines' requirements can be explained within the context of COSO. Even though there is significant overlap in their content, there is also a fundamental difference. While COSO provides many illustrations of what constitutes strong internal control, it does not mandate specific actions. However, the Guidelines contain explicit requirements for an effective program. The following discussion will demonstrate that: (1) the seven minimum requirements of the Guidelines can be found within the COSO evaluation system, and (2) internal auditors who utilize a COSO framework already understand the basics of the Guidelines.

COSO's five components of internal control provide a format to analyze the Guidelines' similarity with COSO. Tables 3-1 through 3-5 highlight the major comparisons. Most of the analysis deals with the Guidelines' requirements for an effective compliance program (FSG#1-7), but the tables also include other relevant sections from the Guidelines.

Control Environment

COSO defines the control environment as the foundation for all of the other internal control components. This environment strongly influences how business activities are structured. The relevant factors for Guidelines' comparisons are: (1) setting the tone at the top, (2) integrity and values, and (3) human resource questions.

COSO encourages organizations to "set the tone at the top." Management should create an atmosphere in which employees can succeed through ethical behavior. (See Appendix C, *A Letter From the Chairman of Sears*.) Management should lead by example, and reward ethical conduct while punishing improper actions. The Guidelines contain several analogous provisions. Organizations with top managers who know about, tolerate, or condone illegal activity will be subject to fines. A company may also qualify for fine reductions if top management cooperates with an investigation, self-reports, and accepts responsibility for the organization's acts. The Guidelines' due diligence requirement states that fine reductions will not be awarded to companies with only a "paper" commitment to compliance. Managers must correct unethical behavior both through words and actions.

The final similarity deals with the Guidelines' requirement of having a top-level official oversee the compliance program. Having a high ranking officer champion the program gives the compliance effort credibility. This champion helps establish the "tone at the top," and signals to employees that compliance and ethics are not just the buzzwords of the month.

Table 3-1
Control Environment

COSO	GUIDELINES
• Management should set the "tone at the top." • Management leads by actions.	• Sanctions if top management knew, tolerated, or condoned improper conduct. • Rewards for cooperation and contrition. • "Due diligence" requirement. • Upper management oversight of compliance program (FSG#2).

• Integrity and ethical values.
  • Code of ethics.
  • Mechanism to encourage employee reporting.
	• Code of ethics (FSG#4).
	• Additional reporting mechanisms (FSG#5).

• Human Resources.
  • Hiring those with evidence of integrity.
  • Consistent discipline.
	• Do not delegate to those with criminal tendencies (FSG#3).
	• Consistent discipline (FSG#6).

COSO has also identified integrity and ethical values as major factors within the control environment. Auditors conducting a COSO evaluation should address certain concerns. Does the organization have a code of ethics? Is there a method for employees to report suspected violations? These COSO considerations are explicitly required in the Guidelines. The Guidelines mandate that an organization must have a method for communicating its standards and procedures to all employees and agents (FSG#4). This can be accomplished with either codes of ethics or training.[1] The Guidelines also call for an additional reporting mechanism in which an employee can report violations without fear of retaliation (FSG#5).

COSO's human resources section of the control environment includes: (1) only hiring employees with evidence of integrity and ethical behavior, and (2) disciplinary actions that send a message that violations will not be tolerated. FSG#3 states that an organization cannot delegate substantial authority to a person with a propensity to engage in illegal activity. Complying with COSO's recommendation of hiring ethical employees will also satisfy FSG#3.

COSO encourages discipline that deters violations. This deterrence will be most effective if employees observe its consistent administration (FSG#6). Without consistent discipline, organizations establish a two-tiered system of justice. Will top managers wink at problems from favored friends, or will everyone receive the same, fair treatment? Many of the Guidelines' requirements can be satisfied by complying with this COSO section.

Risk Assessment

Risk assessment involves the identification and analysis of relevant risks and a strategy to minimize them. Before identifying risks, an organization must establish objectives. These should reflect the nature of the business, industry, and economic environment. Risk management is addressed in the Guidelines' goals section. The Guidelines require an organization to maintain an internal mechanism for preventing, detecting, and reporting violations.

Table 3-2
Risk Assessment

COSO	GUIDELINES
• Objectives related to operations. financial reporting, and compliance. • Identification and analysis of relevant risks. • A strategy to manage risks.	• Provide incentives to maintain internal controls. • Organization must identify whether there are any industry-specific risks.

[1]Appendix C contains as an example the Sears Freedom and Obligations packages. Included within this package is a statement on Shared Beliefs, Leadership Principles, and their Code of Business Conduct.

COSO describes: (1) external risks, such as changes in technology, legislation, or the economy, and (2) internal risks, such as changes in personnel, operating systems, or products. The Guidelines are an example of an external risk due to changes in legislation which can have a significant impact on the organization. To satisfy COSO's risk provision, auditors should be very familiar with the Guidelines, as well as other relevant legislation.

COSO's third factor in risk assessment deals with the organization developing strategies to minimize the risks. The Guidelines call for a similar process. They require organizations to evaluate inherent business risks and take steps to minimize them. For example, if an organization's sales force has substantial discretion in setting prices, the organization must have controls in place to prevent and detect possible price-fixing. The COSO risk assessment process of objective setting, risk identification and evaluation, and strategy setting must occur for the Guidelines to be satisfied.

Control Activities

Control activities are the policies and procedures that help ensure management's directives are followed. One of management's directives is to comply with laws, therefore the Guidelines fall within COSO's broader perspective. One specific Guideline requirement is that organizations must have compliance procedures that are reasonably capable of reducing criminal conduct. This may be accomplished by control activities which include approvals, authorizations, reconciliations, and segregation of duties.

This process requires continuous improvement. Management should monitor and evaluate control activities, as well as make any necessary revisions. When a control failure is identified, both COSO and the Guidelines indicate a change may be necessary. Under COSO, one would assess the risks related to additional failures, and then design preventive policies and procedures. FSG#7 requires organizations to explain the modifications they have made and why these will prevent similar violations in the future.

Information and Communication

Information systems deal with external and internal sources, financial and non-financial information, and should assist management in achieving its objectives. COSO emphasizes that all personnel must understand their role in the internal control system, and have a means of communicating significant information upstream. Effective communications should flow up, down, across, and even outside the organization.

The Guidelines' analogous requirements are found in FSG#4 and FSG#5. FSG#4 states that the organization must have taken steps to effectively communicate its standards and procedures to all employees and other agents by requiring participation

Table 3-3
Control Activities

COSO	GUIDELINES
• Policies and procedures to help ensure that management's directives are followed.	• Establish standards and procedures that are capable of reducing the prospect of criminal conduct (FSG#1). • After violations occur, determine what modifications need to be made to prevent future problems (FSG#7).

Table 3-4
Information and Communication

COSO	GUIDELINES
• Pertinent information must be identified, captured, and communicated in an appropriate format and time frame.	• Must take steps to communicate effectively its standards and procedures to all employees and other agents (FSG#4). • Required training or publications (FSG#4). • Establish additional reporting mechanisms (such as Hotlines, Helplines) (FSG#5).

in training programs or by distributing publications (i.e., codes of ethics) explaining the company's standard of conduct.

Effective managers must not only communicate corporate policy, they must also be good listeners and act upon their employees' concerns. FSG#5 states that employees need a non-threatening way of communicating their concerns without fear of reprisal. Organizations should create an environment in which information can flow uphill from the employees to upper management. To handle situations when the traditional reporting method to your supervisor is inappropriate, many companies have established additional reporting mechanisms (i.e., "Hotlines," "Helplines," or "Openlines"). A non-threatening additional reporting mechanism is the type of open dialogue between the company and its employees which will satisfy both COSO and the Guidelines.

Monitoring

The monitoring process assesses the quality of an internal control system's performance over time. It involves both ongoing activities and separate evaluations. The need for separate evaluations depends on the assessment of risks and the effectiveness of the ongoing monitoring. COSO states that deficiencies in internal controls should be reported upstream. Serious matters must be reported to top management and the board. FSG#5 calls for organizations to monitor and audit systems that are reasonably designed to detect criminal conduct by its employees and other agents. While the previous comparisons between COSO and the Guidelines have been very similar, the monitoring component provides a near identical fit.

Table 3-5
Monitoring

COSO	GUIDELINES
• Ongoing assessment of the internal control system.	• Utilize monitoring and auditing systems designed to detect criminal conduct (FSG#5).

Conclusion

Internal auditors can play an important role in minimizing any possible federal fines because of their organizational role and position. The COSO report designates internal auditors as being significantly responsible for evaluating the effectiveness of the internal control and contributing to its ongoing effectiveness. The COSO integrated framework can act as the road map for gaining an understanding of the importance and requirement of the Guidelines.

CHAPTER 4
THE SURVEY

To investigate the impact of the Federal Sentencing Guidelines on internal auditors, information was obtained from a review of the related literature, interviews with leaders of internal auditing departments, interviews with directors of compliance programs, and responses of internal auditors and compliance officers to a nationwide survey. The review of the literature and the interviews were used to design a survey instrument to obtain information from a broad audience of internal auditors.

The survey was conducted with the assistance of The Institute of Internal Auditors Research Foundation. This chapter discusses the survey method, demographics, and overall findings. Additional findings are included in other sections of the report. Copies of the survey instruments are included in Appendix A, and Appendix B provides additional details and statistical analysis of the survey responses.

Survey Method

Questionnaires were mailed to a group of individuals selected from the membership records of The Institute of Internal Auditors (IIA). The group selected identified themselves in The IIA database as the highest-level internal auditors for their organization (typically, vice presidents). This group would likely be the most knowledgeable about the Federal Sentencing Guidelines and its potential impact on internal auditing. This group represented 469 individuals at the time of the survey, and questionnaires were mailed to the entire group. Individuals receiving a survey were also asked to deliver an additional questionnaire to another person within their organization who had general responsibility for compliance questions. Since not all organizations have compliance officers, the response rate from compliance officers was approximately half that of internal auditors. From those surveyed, responses were received from 129 internal auditors and 62 compliance officers.

Demographic Information

Participants responded to questions related to organization size, affiliation, and industry identification. These categories helped identify possible response differences based on factors such as size or industry, as well as document the variety of individuals responding to our survey. This section summarizes the demographic information.

Size

Respondents reported the size of their organization in revenues, assets, and number of employees. Table 4-1 displays the means, ranges, and quartile breakdowns for the organizational size variables based on the responses of the internal auditors.

Organizational Affiliation

Two particular organizations were separately identified: the Business Roundtable and the Defense Industry Initiative Signatories (DIIS). Approximately 34% of the group (48 of the 142 responding organizations) was associated with the Business Roundtable. Only 3% (4 of the 142 responding organizations) indicated that their organization was a DIIS. (In 1996, the total number of DIIS was only 50.)

Industry

Respondents provided descriptions of their industries (such as manufacturing or banking) which were used to categorize organizations into eight industrial groups.[1] As shown in Table 4-2, the largest groups of respondents were from the manufacturing and the finance/insurance industries, with each of those two groups representing more than 20% of all responses.

[1]The eight categories were chosen to correspond with prior research on ethics policies and procedures in "Ethics Policies and Programs in American Business" by the Ethics Resource Center (1990).

Table 4-1
Organization Size

	Revenues (in millions)	Assets (in millions)	Employees
Mean	$4,844	$13,930	17,835
Range			
Minimum	$3	$70	36
Maximum	$63,000	$217,000	250,000
Quartiles			
1st	$3 - $950	$70 - $1,467	36 - 3400
2nd	$1,000 - $2,705	$1,500 - $4,000	3,500 - 8,000
3rd	$2,800 - $4,200	$4,500 - $11,000	8,500 - 22,000
4th	$5,000 - $63,000	$11,700 - $217,000	24,000 - 250,000

Table 4-2
Industry Representation

	Number of Respondents	Percentage of Respondents
Manufacturing	34	26.6%
Finance, Insurance*	30	23.4%
Agriculture, Forestry, Fishing, Mining	16	12.5%
Transportation, Communications, Public Utilities	15	11.7%
Services	9	7.0%
Retail Trade	6	4.7%
Wholesale Trade	2	1.6%
Construction	1	.8%
Not Reported	15	11.7%
Total	128	100%

*Of the 30 respondents, 22 were in finance (banking, financial services) and eight were in the insurance industry.

Individual Demographics

The demographic information on the individual internal auditing respondents indicated that the mean respondent was 46 years old, with 13 years of internal auditing experience, and 23 years of total work experience. More than 89% of the respondents were male. Of the respondents, 59% (76) were CPAs, 30% (39) were CIAs, and 31% (40) indicated other certifications (CBA, CMA, etc.).

Survey Results

Respondents generally were familiar with the Guidelines, with an average rating of 3.34 for internal auditors and 3.84 for compliance officers, based on a 5-point scale from "Not Familiar" (1) to "Extremely Familiar" (5). As shown in Figure 4-1, 56% of the internal auditors and 72% of the compliance officers indicated that their familiarity was a "4" or a "5." Only 10% of all respondents indicated that they were not familiar with the Guidelines.

Figure 4-1
Level of Familiarity with the Guidelines
Internal Auditors and Compliance Officers

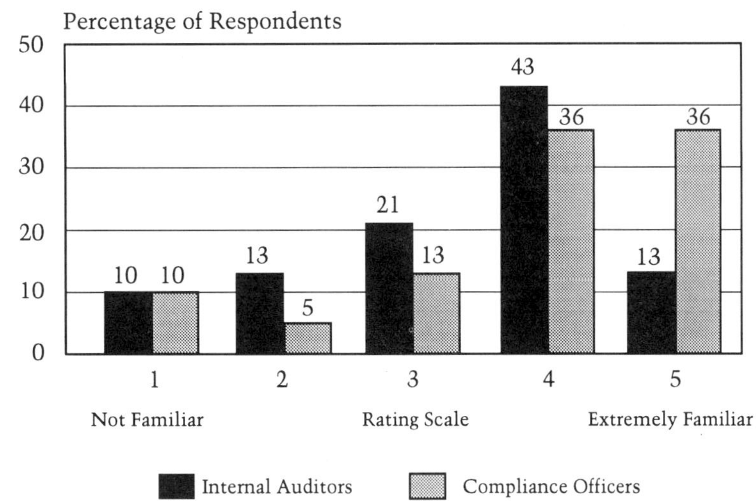

When asked about the potential impact of the Guidelines on their organizations, respondents were not convinced that it would be significant. This seemed to confirm prior interview comments obtained by the researchers. For example, some of the interviewees in regulated industries were very familiar with the Guidelines. They did not anticipate any significant impact to their organization because their organizations had programs which met the Guidelines' requirements for an effective compliance program. Some internal auditors, with some familiarity with the Guidelines, were not sure whether the Guidelines would have any impact on them because their organization did not have "direct dealings with the Federal Government."

Figure 4-2 shows that only 3% of internal auditors and 5% of compliance officers indicated a significant impact. For internal auditors, 10% expected no impact, and 9% of compliance officers expected no impact. The mean ratings were 2.7 for internal auditors and 3.1 for compliance officers, based on a 5-point scale with "1" as "No Impact" and "5" as "Significant Impact."

Respondents were asked to indicate key characteristics from a list of items that influenced their perception of the potential impact of the Guidelines on their organizations. Of the 129 respondents, 38% (49 of 129) cited as a reason for the perceived impact "an analysis by the legal depart-

Figure 4-2
Perceived Impact of Guidelines
Internal Auditors and Compliance Officers

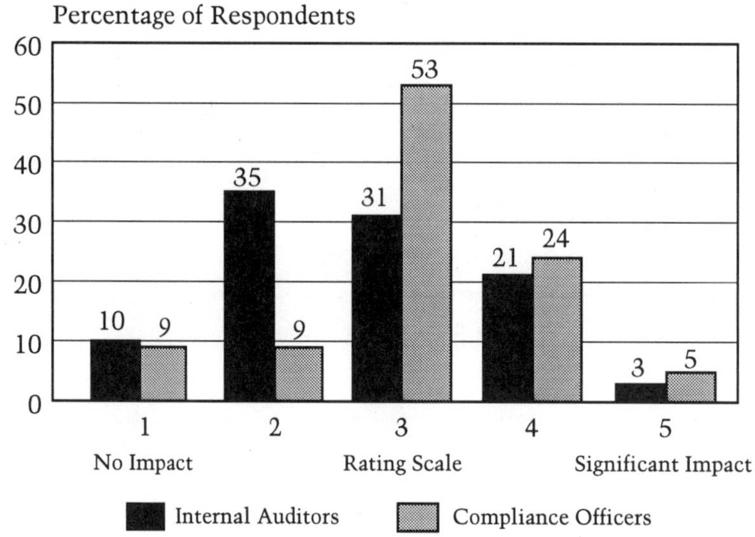

ment." Almost 35% (45 of 129) indicated that federal, state, or industry regulations already satisfied the requirements.

Based on prior interviews, it was expected that the internal auditing department would play several roles regarding their organization's compliance program. As shown in Figure 4-3, about 30% of the respondents indicated that key members from internal auditing participated in compliance committees within their organization. Eleven respondents (9%) indicated that there was no compliance program at their organization, while 17 respondents (14%) indicated that internal auditing was the compliance program. A number of respondents indicated that in their organizations, internal auditing monitors (audits/evaluates) the compliance program.

Figure 4-3
Internal Audit Involvement in the
Overall Compliance Program (CP)

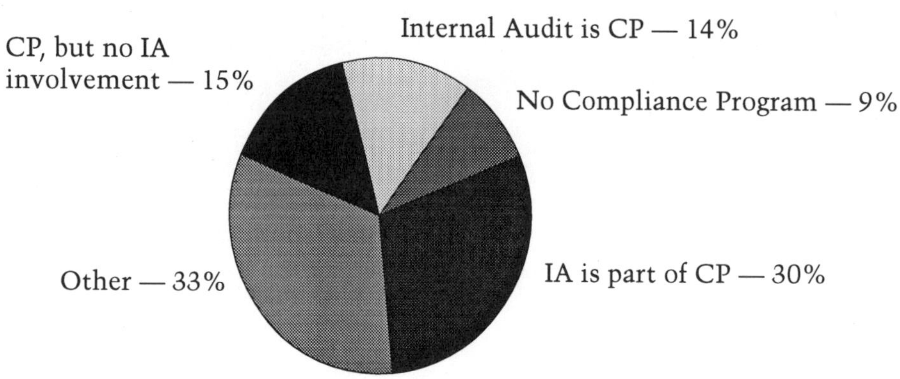

Respondents were asked to rate their organization on compliance with the seven minimum criteria established by the Federal Sentencing Guidelines. The mean scores on a 5-point scale (1 = "Very Low", 5 = "Very High") are presented in Figure 4-4. The mean responses on the seven items for internal auditors ranged from 3.32 to 3.86. For compliance officers, the mean responses ranged from 3.38 to 4.1. These means are referenced in Chapters 5-11 which provide discussions of the seven requirements.

Comparisons were made of mean scores based on characteristics of the organization. The mean scores on rating compliance with the seven minimum requirements were higher for Business Roundtable members and for large organizations. Industry mean scores were investigated, but in this study no significant differences were found. Mean scores were also observed to be different based on the involvement of internal auditing in the compliance program. Internal auditing involvement resulted in higher mean scores. Additional analysis of the survey responses are reported in Appendix B.

Figure 4-4
Perceived Compliance with Requirements
Internal Auditors and Compliance Officers

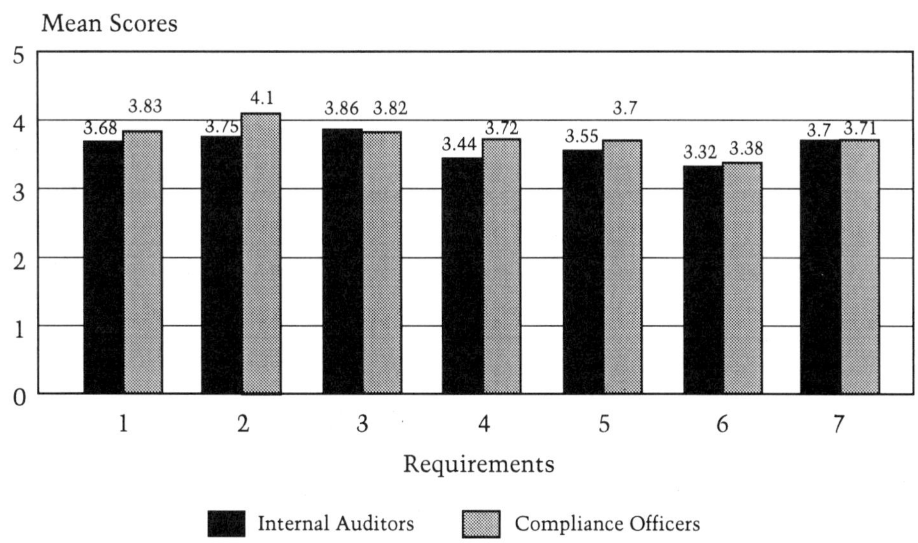

CHAPTER 5
REQUIREMENT #1

"The organization must have established compliance standards and procedures to be followed by its employees and other agents that are reasonably capable of reducing the prospect of criminal conduct." — (FSG#1)

Introduction

This requirement specifically calls for policies and procedures to reduce the prospect of criminal conduct. The compliance program should be tailored to the organization's business operations. The starting point of any compliance program is to conduct a risk assessment and determine where the company has legal exposure. Certain risks are industry specific. For example, a securities broker must avoid violations of insider trading laws, a defense contractor must carefully watch procurement processes, and a company involved in foreign sales must comply with the Foreign Corrupt Practices Act. Other risks such as price fixing, fraud, and environmental violations span many industries. Additional concerns addressed by compliance programs include: (1) conflicts of interest, (2) bribes and kickbacks, (3) gifts and entertainment, (4) antidiscrimination policies, and (5) occupational health/safety.[1] Typical corporate responses addressing these concerns include: (1) establishing standard operating procedures, (2) restricting access to activities, (3) developing codes of conduct, and (4) providing hotlines.

Survey Results

Based on survey results, internal auditors and compliance officers generally consider their current status on this requirement to be better than average. On a 5 point scale, with 5 indicating a very high rating of current compliance with the requirement, internal auditor responses resulted in a mean score of 3.68, while compliance officers report a mean of 3.83. The frequency of responses, as shown in Figure 5-1, illustrates that very few respondents gave their program a below average score.

Role of the Internal Auditor

Based on the authors' surveys, many internal auditors are involved in activities related to the design, monitoring, and investigation of reported failures dealing with compliance programs. Figure 5-2 displays the frequency distribution of responses related to internal auditor activities. Considering reported values of "4" or "5" as significant (5-point scale, with "5" indicating "very involved"), over 43% of respondents reported significant involvement in design activities, over 67% reported significant involvement in monitoring activities, and over 70% reported significant involvement in activities related to the investigation of reported failures.

When asked to provide highly effective or unique practices on the survey, the internal auditor's responses included the following items:

Involvement in Personnel Decisions:
- Audit Director must review all terminations "for cause" prior to action to determine the extent of the investigation.
- Post-employment screening.
- Preemployment screening.

Obtaining Statements regarding Compliance:
- Annual Ethics Compliance Questionnaire (by internal auditing).
- On all audits, senior management must sign a statement saying they have read and

[1]See Appendix C for topics included within Sears Code of Business Conduct.

Figure 5-1
Assessment of Compliance with FSG#1
(Percentage of Responses by Group)

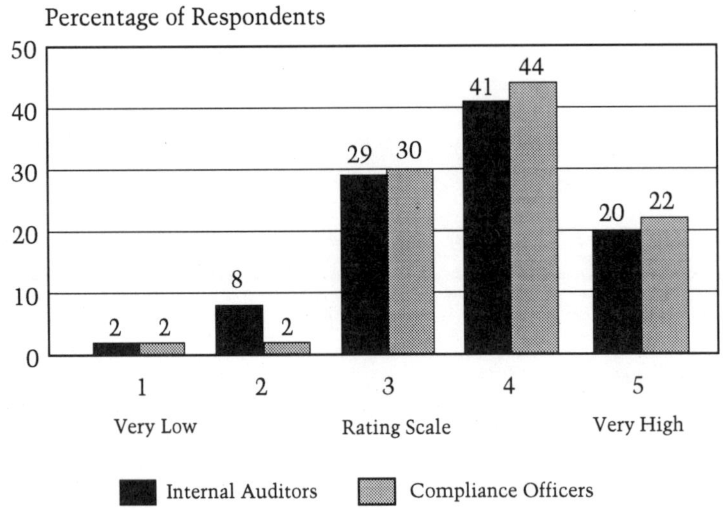

FSG#1: "The organization must have established compliance standards and procedures to be followed by its employees and other agents that are reasonably capable of reducing the prospect of criminal conduct."

Figure 5-2 (FSG#1)
Internal Audit Involvement with Design, Monitoring, and Investigation Activities

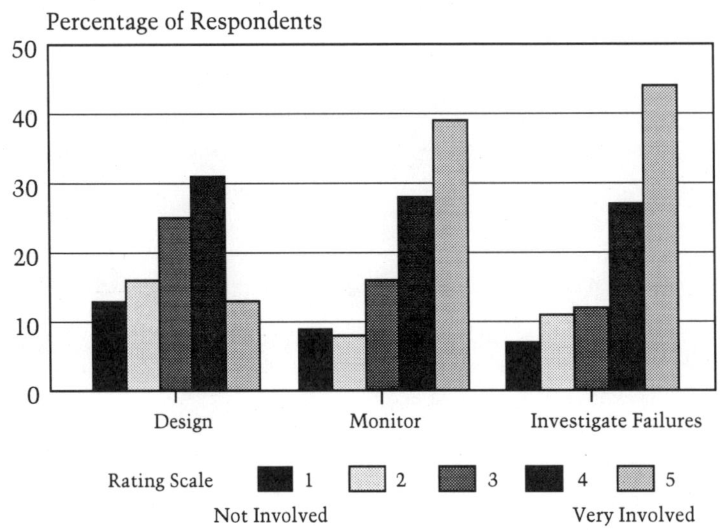

are familiar with the company's code of ethics and that they are not aware of any violations of the code.

Monitoring the Compliance Program:
- We audit the compliance program.
- Compliance program monitored by legal and internal audit.
- Annual attestation of the compliance program.
- Required self-audits by each operating entity, by individuals independent of daily activity or control with results reported to a central monitoring area. The self audits include control issues and regulators' compliance issues.
- All audits have significant compliance features.
- We have a self-review program at each company location with follow-up and compliance review by internal audit.

Designing the Compliance Program
- In our decentralized organization, each business unit has their own compliance program. Internal audit is currently involved in developing a more centralized corporate level process.

These items continue to illustrate the involvement of internal auditors in various aspects of a compliance program designed to reduce the prospect of criminal conduct.

Business Considerations

The final section of this chapter presents a list of questions to assist in the evaluation of FSG #1 for your organization.

Q1. Has your organization conducted a risk assessment to determine the level of exposure on different concerns?

A. Yes____ No____

Q2. What policies and procedures has your organization implemented to minimize the identified risks?

A. Documenting the process of determining relevant risks and the corresponding corrective actions to address these risks can be critical in obtaining fine reductions.

Q3. Was the risk assessment and policy promulgation conducted before or after the instant offense was investigated?

A. The only organizations that would be seeking fine reductions are those which have had a violation. While it is clear that the organization's compliance program did not prevent the instant offense, courts will measure a program based upon management's due diligence, not perfection. One of the factors in analyzing due diligence will be the timing of the program. Compliance programs developed post-offense, but pre-sentencing will probably not receive much credit.

Q4. Is your organization a member of any industry groups chartered to exchange "best practices" to limit violations?

A. One of the best examples of an industry group that exchanges best practices to prevent violations is defense contractors. This group has 50 "signatories" to the Defense Industry Initiative. These signatories send representatives to an annual "Best Practices Forum" and exchange ideas about what policies and procedures have been effective. In addition, the Conference Board sponsors an annual Business Ethics Conference in which participants from many diverse industries exchange their best practices. Industry groups and conferences can be very productive, but representatives must be cautioned to limit their discussions to compliance questions and not to discuss any matters which have anti-trust implications.

CHAPTER 6
REQUIREMENT #2

"Specific individual(s) within high-level personnel of the organization must have been assigned overall responsibility to oversee compliance with such standards and procedures." — (FSG #2)

Introduction

This section explains the oversight and stewardship requirements organizations must meet in their compliance processes. This can range from a formal ethics officer or ombudsman, to increased responsibilities for the general auditor, corporate counsel, or human resource officer. Assigning the compliance program to a current employee is especially common for smaller organizations that may lack the funding for a separate compliance office or even a compliance officer. While specific positions are not a prerequisite for qualifying for fine reductions, organizations without designated compliance personnel may require additional documentation and explanation concerning how their organizational efforts satisfy this requirement.

Survey Results

The survey indicated that internal auditors and compliance officers generally rated their organization's current compliance fairly high. The mean scores were 3.75 for internal auditors and 4.10 for compliance officers, using a 5-point scale with 5 indicating a very high rating. As compared to the ratings of the other seven requirements, this was the highest rating given by compliance officers and the second highest for internal auditors. Figure 6-1 displays the frequency distributions for both response groups. Not surprisingly, very few compliance officers gave a low rating to this item, given that the organization had identified them to complete this compliance officer questionnaire. Approximately 80% of the compliance officers rated their organizations toward the top of the scale. Internal auditors' responses were generally positive.

Figure 6-1
Assessment of Compliance with FSG#2
(Percentage of Responses by Group)

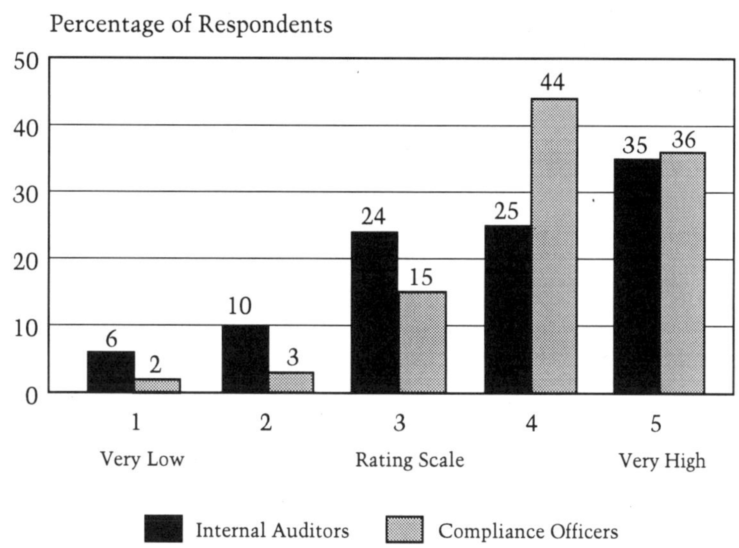

The survey instrument also asked respondents to identify whether an individual or a committee had been designated as responsible for the compliance function. Approximately 60% indicated that an individual was responsible for the program while 40% indicated that a committee was in charge of compliance. When an individual was specifically identified, it was most likely to be a compliance officer or someone in the legal department as shown in Figure 6-2. Slightly over 52% of the respondents who indicated that a committee was in charge pointed to a standing committee of top management. Of the remainder indicating committee oversight, 36% reported that a special committee had been designated for this purpose.

Figure 6-2
Individuals and Committees Responsible for the Compliance Program

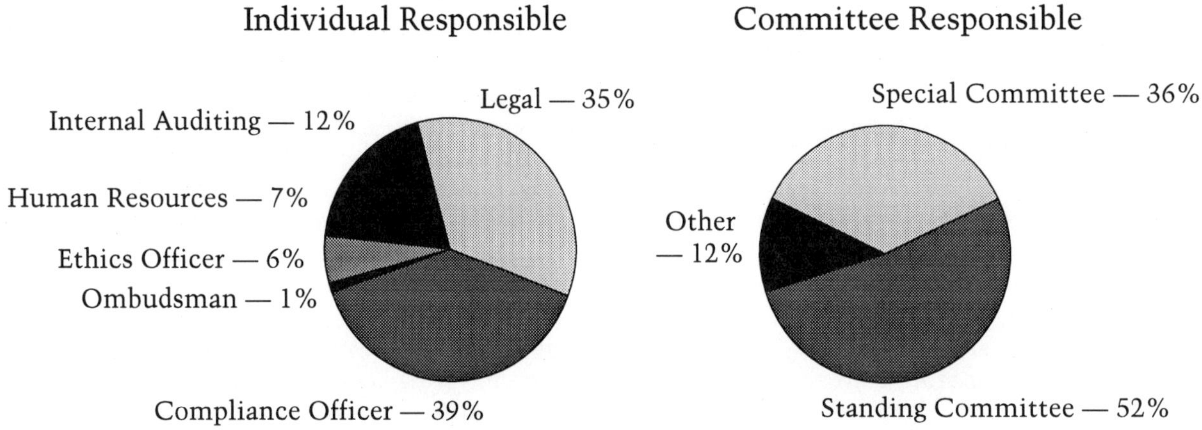

Role of the Internal Auditor

The survey instrument asked respondents to indicate their involvement in the oversight of the compliance program. Three alternatives were selected by respondents: (1) member of the oversight committee, (2) not involved, or (3) other involvement. As shown in Figure 6-3, 35% of respondents indicated involvement as a member of the committee. Also, 28% indicated no involvement. Of the 38% indicating other involvement, the explanations varied. Many indicated that internal auditing was responsible for auditing the program.

Figure 6-3
Oversight Role of Internal Audit

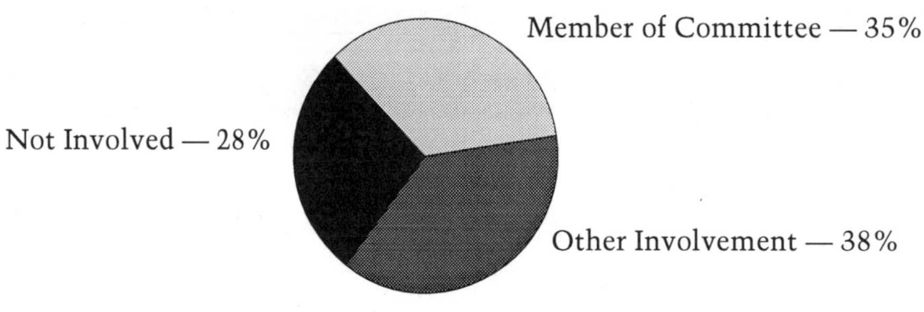

Common Practices

Larger organizations often satisfy this requirement with compliance officers or ombudsmen, and an increasing number of organizations designate ethics officers. These individuals are often associated with groups like: (1) the Ethics Officer Association (EOA) (based at Bentley College), (2) the Defense Industry Initiative (with 50 major defense contractors as signatories), and (3) the Ombudsmen Association. Members within these organizations maintain contact and often exchange "best practices" regarding compliance issues.

Participation and incorporation of these best practices also help satisfy another Guidelines requirement, "Section 8A1.2,... states an organization's failure to incorporate and follow applicable industry practice... weighs against a finding of an effective program to prevent and detect violations of law."

Business Considerations

The final section of this chapter presents a list of questions and a discussion of their importance. They provide assistance in the evaluation of FSG#2 within organizations.

Q1. Is your organization considering establishing a separate office dealing with compliance issues, or expanding the duties of existing functions (i.e., Auditing, Legal, Security, Human Resources)?

A. It may be financially impractical to establish a separate position or department dealing with compliance issues. Your organization may not have a sufficient volume of concerns that would justify a standalone office. This would be an adequate explanation for having the compliance function absorbed by existing departments. Larger organizations with more frequent allegations must question the efficacy of adding these duties to professionals who are already strapped for time. Will these busy professionals be able to address these questions adequately, or will questions of compliance be marginalized as an afterthought, only receiving attention on a crisis-by-crisis basis? If this latter scenario is the case, organizations will be hard pressed to argue that they had an effective program to prevent and detect violations.

Q2. Does your organization send any implicit or explicit messages to employees if it appears that your organization is unwilling to commit resources to compliance questions?

A. Even with adequate resources dedicated to compliance questions, organizations must convince employees that they are not merely throwing money at the problem with hopes that it will go away. Compliance programs will gain employee acceptance after employees understand its use and believe that it is meant to help, not threaten, them. Organizations that are either unwilling or unable to allocate resources to compliance programs will have a more difficult time gaining employee acceptance. Management must do more than "Just say no to code violations," it must back up these slogans with appropriate financial support.

Q3. If your organization establishes a separate compliance position or office, should the person heading that effort come from within or outside the company?

A. The question about whether an internal or external candidate should head the organization's compliance efforts can be the cause for intense debate. Internal candidates with a reputation for integrity can immediately engender confidence by employees. Candidates who are either unknown or not respected can create distrust for the position, which may never be overcome.

B. External candidates may not know the culture of the organization. While this can provide a fresh perspective, "outsiders" must avoid the appearance that theirs is the better position because that is how they did it in their former organization. Once a balance is achieved, the compliance officer will develop trust based upon their current actions, not their war stories.

Q4. Is there a perceived difference between compliance officers, ethics officers, and ombudsmen? If so, which position would work best within the organization?

A. While it may appear to be a question of semantics, the title of this officer may send different signals to the organization. Compliance officers conjure up an image of a person who is well versed in laws and regulations. Their job is to make sure that these same laws and regulations are not violated.

B. The title "Ethics Officer" presents a very different picture. An ethics officer, while being conversant in laws and regulations, is not driven by them. The organization's core values would provide the benchmark for measurement of success, not an outside agency's proclamations. While complying with laws and regulations would be a given for ethics officers, they may move the organization to try and satisfy a more inspirational standard.

C. Ombudsmen seem to occupy a different role. The traditional model views an ombudsman as a designated neutral who places a premium on the confidential nature of the communication between employees and their office. This is not necessarily the case with compliance officers. As neutrals, ombudsmen neither represent management nor the employees. They act as resources of information and provide additional avenues for troubled employees to resolve their conflicts. The strong hope is that their reputation for neutrality and confidentiality will encourage employees who are discouraged by traditional methods of handling complaints to come forward with potentially difficult questions.

Q5. Is information gathered by this officer subject to any privilege that would protect it from subpoena?

A. See Chapter 12 for a discussion regarding workpaper privilege.

Q6. Does your organization's chief compliance officer/ethics officer/ombudsman have direct access to the board of directors?

A. It may be very helpful to establish a separate subcommittee of the board of directors which deals exclusively with compliance questions. Having this committee staffed with outside directors would improve the appearance of the committee's independence.

CHAPTER 7
REQUIREMENT #3

"The organization must have used due care not to delegate substantial discretionary authority to individuals who the organization knew, or should have known through the exercise of due diligence, had a propensity to engage in illegal activity." — (FSG#3)

Introduction

This requirement addresses the importance of establishing policies and procedures to identify employees with a propensity to engage in illegal acts and to avoid placing those employees in sensitive positions. Background investigations of job applicants should include reference letters, letters from prior employers, verification of credentials, and other appropriate information. Assignment of additional responsibilities to current employees should also be based on careful assessment of their past history. The requirement specifically calls for policies to reduce the prospect of criminal conduct.

These same policies and procedures can also be used to avoid lawsuits under common law theories of negligent hiring, negligent training, and negligent retention. Background checks can prove very frustrating to the hiring employer. Fearing defamation lawsuits, employers merely verify dates of employment for their ex-employees.

Several states have responded to employers' frustration in being denied access to this information by proposing legislation that would give terminating employers a statutorily qualified privilege to disclose information about their ex-employees. This increased protection will promote the freer flow of information by making it more difficult for ex-employees to sue.

In addition to reference checking for previous violations, employers can monitor employees' current behavior to determine whether there are any indicators of a propensity to engage in illegal activity. This can include: (1) monitoring business-related telephone calls, (2) scanning e-mail messages, and (3) placing surveillance cameras in the workplace. These practices will be more likely to survive judicial and employee scrutiny if employees are informed about, and agree to, these practices beforehand.

Survey Results

Based on the survey, internal auditors and compliance officers generally consider their current status on this requirement to be very good. On a 5 point scale, with 5 indicating a very high rating of current compliance with the requirement, internal auditor responses resulted in a mean score of 3.86, while compliance officers report a mean of 3.82. This was the highest mean rating given by the internal auditors and the third highest for compliance officers. The frequency of responses, as shown in Figure 7-1, illustrates that few respondents gave their program a below average score.

Role of the Internal Auditor

The role of the internal auditor regarding this item varies considerably. Based on our interviews, internal auditors may be involved in activities related to the design, monitoring, and investigation of reported failures. Figure 7-2 illustrates the frequency distribution of responses related to internal auditor activities. Considering reported values of "4" or "5" as significant (5-point scale with "5" indicating "very involved"), 38% of respondents reported significant involvement in design activities, 57% reported significant involvement in monitoring activities, and 69% reported significant involvement in activities related to the investigation of reported failures.

Figure 7-1
Assessment of Compliance with FSG#3
(Percentage of Responses by Group)

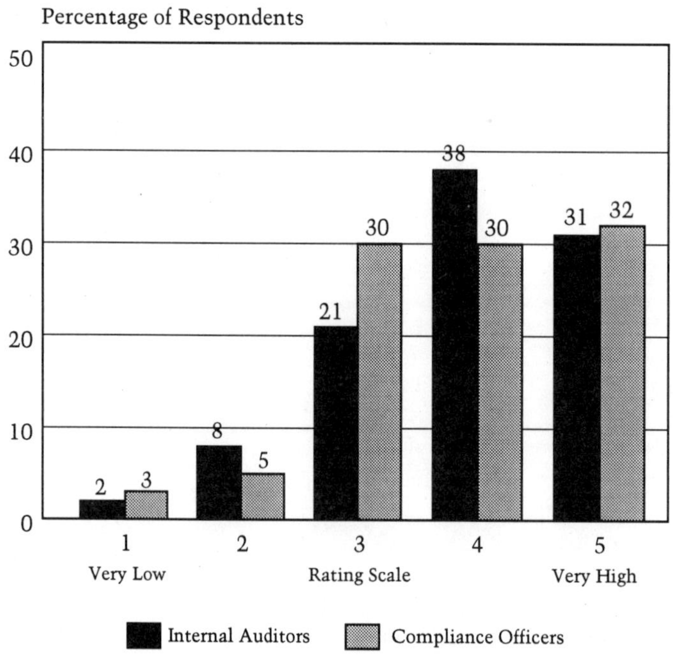

FSG#3: "The organization must have used due care not to delegate substantial discretionary authority to individuals who the organization knew, or should have known through the exercise of due diligence, had a propensity to engage in illegal activity."

Figure 7-2 (FSG#3)
Internal Audit Involvement with Design, Monitoring, and Investigation Activities

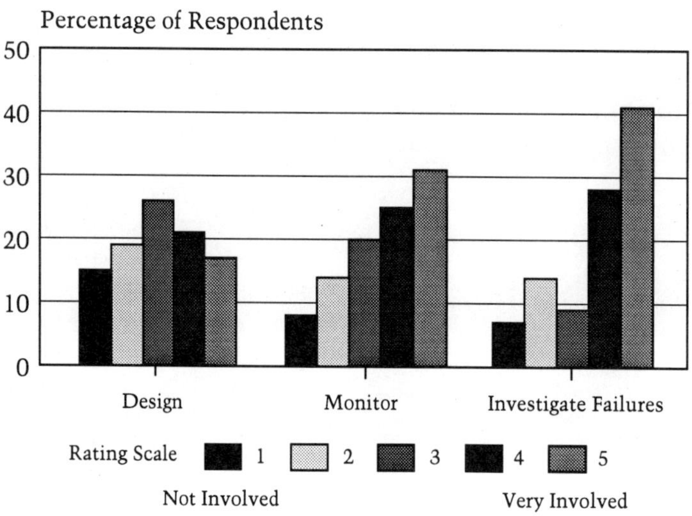

When asked to provide highly effective or unique practices, the following items were identified:

- Preemployment screening.
- Additional background checks for certain positions and divisions.
- Strict authority levels.
- Strong segregation of duties to minimize individual discretionary authority.
- Review of all accusations of wrongdoing and all disciplinary actions.

These items continue to illustrate the involvement of internal auditors in various aspects of a compliance program.

Business Considerations

The final section of this chapter presents a list of questions to assist in the evaluation of FSG#3.

Q1. Does your organization perform some form of reference checking on prospective employees?

A. Failure to perform a reference check may cause the employer to be sued for negligent hiring, had the violation been foreseeable and preventable by conducting a thorough background investigation.

Q2. Does your organization obtain releases from former employees authorizing the company to provide accurate information to prospective employers?

A. Releases obtained from ex-employees may not prevent every claim of defamation. They should still be considered because releases increase the organization's odds of winning future lawsuits.

Q3. Are there any files documenting that applicants were not hired or employees were not promoted to positions of substantial authority because it was determined that they had a propensity to engage in illegal activity?

A. Organizations should accurately and adequately document their actions. Accurate documentation includes a document retention policy. Organizations should develop a procedure to review the retained documents and keep the compliance documents in a central location. A retention policy should also include the systematic review and deletion of unnecessary files. This policy becomes very important during investigations and discovery in preparation for litigation. Even if an unnecessary document does not damage the organization, it is very expensive to have managers and attorneys review these files. Unnecessary files take up expensive storage space in a warehouse, valuable disk space on a hard drive, and limited space on your organization's e-mail system.

Employees should also be instructed to limit their comments in reports to verifiable facts. Editorial remarks or attempts at humor can be misconstrued during subsequent investigations.

Q4. Does your organization monitor your employees' telephone calls or e-mail? If so, are employees warned about the possibility of monitoring?

A. Surveillance and monitoring may be an effective way of eliciting information about a current employee's propensity to engage in illegal activity. Organizations must be careful to balance the usefulness of this information against the privacy concerns of their employees. Organizations that monitor telephone calls should only do so long enough to determine if they are business related. Once it is determined to be business related, monitoring may continue. Organizations may prohibit personal calls, but they should tell employees that any business-related telephone calls or e-mail messages may be monitored.

Q5. Does your organization have a policy of removing employees charged with criminal offenses from positions of substantial authority?

A. This was a provision that the government imposed upon NME as part of their settlement (see Chapter 1 for more details on NME). NME also agreed to terminate indicted employees if they were ultimately convicted.

CHAPTER 8
REQUIREMENT #4

"The organization must have taken steps to communicate effectively its standards and procedures to all employees and other agents, e.g., by requiring participation in training programs or by disseminating publications that explain in a practical manner what is required." — (FSG #4)

Introduction

This section of the Guidelines raises the important question, "How will your organization communicate policies to its employees?" Most companies have many channels of communication available to convey their standards and procedures. The effectiveness of these channels, however, may vary. As in its other sections, the Guidelines provide broad concepts, not strict procedures. This Guideline section addresses the use of training programs and publications. One of the more common forms of communicating policies, especially in larger organizations, is the use of a Code of Ethics or Standards of Business Conduct.[1]

Survey Results

Based on survey results, internal auditors and compliance officers generally consider their current status on this requirement to be better than average. Using a 5-point scale, with 5 indicating a very high rating of current compliance with the requirement, internal auditor responses resulted in a mean score of 3.44, while compliance officers reported a mean of 3.72. The frequency of responses, as shown in Figure 8-1, reveals that very few compliance officers gave their program a low score.

Figure 8-1
Assessment of Compliance with FSG#4
(Percentage of Responses by Group)

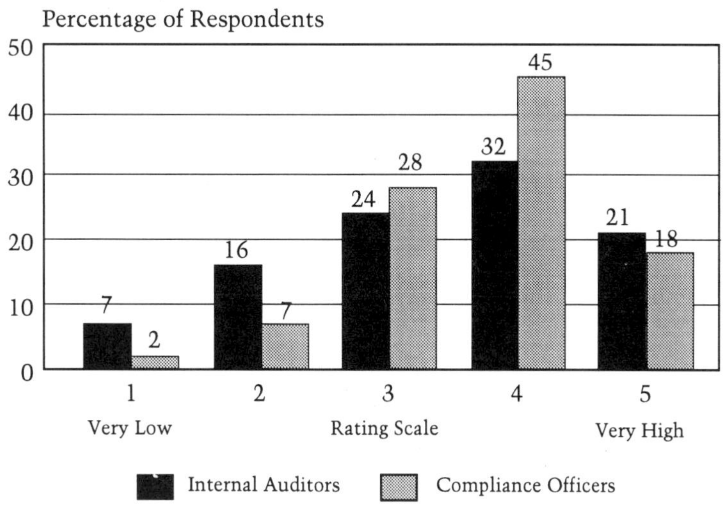

[1]To review a sample Code of Ethics, see Appendix C.

This is not surprising since a program which has identified a compliance officer is more likely to have addressed the need for the communication of policies. Both internal auditors and compliance officers gave a high rating (4 out of 5) as their most frequent response.

Role of the Internal Auditor

The role of the internal auditor regarding this item varies considerably. Based on our interviews, internal auditors may be involved with developing the code of ethics, annually certifying that employees have received and agree to follow the code of conduct, contributing "sanitized" cases (actual cases of wrongdoing, but with names and other identifying factors changed) for training purposes, and monitoring the extensiveness of the training (i.e., Did all employees receive the training?).

Response to the survey indicated that participation in these activities by internal auditors varied as shown in Figure 8-2, with the most extensive involvement related to the certification process and the development of training programs or codes of conduct. The certification process typically involved obtaining annual statements from employees that they have reviewed the code of ethics and have not, or will not, violate the code. The responses also indicated that internal auditors are often involved in the development of the standards of conduct.

However, in our overall responses, more than 20% indicated no involvement in the four specified activities. When the sample was analyzed comparing members of the Business Roundtable to others, it was noted that on all items, internal auditors associated with Business Roundtable organizations reported a higher degree of involvement. This was particularly true in activities related to the development of the code and tracking the certification process of the code. Possible involvement of internal auditors in each of the four previously mentioned activities is discussed below, with an additional section based on the other activities identified through our survey.

Development of the Code

Since internal auditors are often involved with the risk assessment process, they are in a unique position to make sure that the code appropriately addresses the concerns of the business. This role carries through the initial development phase and subsequent reviews.

Figure 8-2
Internal Audit Involvement Related to Codes of Conduct and Training Programs (FSG#4)

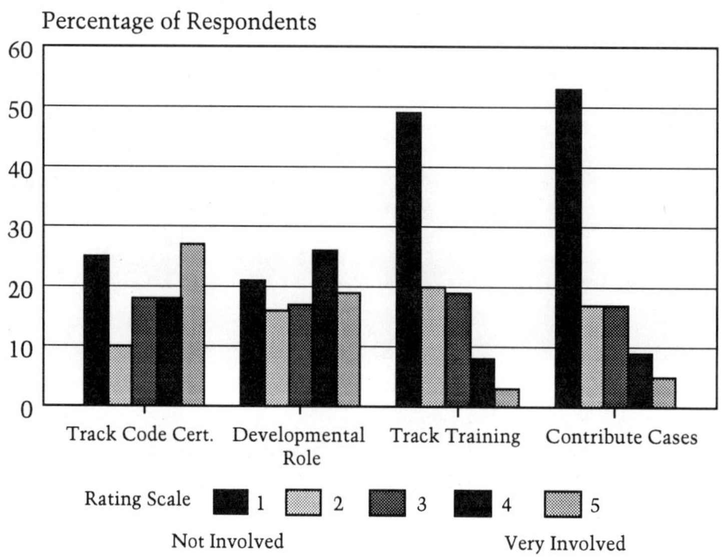

Certification of the Codes

In many organizations, the internal audit function is responsible for obtaining an annual written certification from key individuals indicating that they are aware of the code and have not violated any of its provisions during the past year. Often, the certifications are mailed directly to the internal auditing department and any omissions are pursued. A missing certification report may simply be the result of a busy manager overlooking the report, or it may signal a problem that needs investigating.

Development of Training Programs

In the same manner that internal auditors can provide a significant contribution to the development of the code, they can also assist in the development of training programs. The programs may be general in nature, such as a training program or orientation session for all new employees, or the programs may respond to a specific need, such as a training session for processing electronic transactions. Training may be both proactive and reactive in nature. Proactive sessions are desirable for addressing anticipated problems. Yet, reactive sessions in response to identified problems are also valuable.

Tracking Participation in Training Programs

Many organizations require certain training programs for all employees, or specific training programs to be completed for certain groups of employees. Often, the internal audit function is given the responsibility for tracking participation in the required training and reporting any exceptions. This type of record keeping can assist in documenting an organization's attempts to communicate policies and procedures to employees.

Contribution of "Sanitized Cases"

As noted above, proactive training is desirable, but reactive training also serves a valuable purpose. If an organization has detected problems, the specific case facts may be useful in future training programs. In some organizations, the names and other identifying factors are changed and the "sanitized" version of the case is circulated within organization publications as an example of potential problems, or the case may be used in training activities. In some highly publicized cases, the actual names and facts are used.

Other Involvement

In addition, internal auditors identified other related activities on our survey. Specifically noted were: involvement in preparation of training videos to be shown to all new employees; certification related to conflicts of interest; and preparation of an annual "termination for cause" report. These activities, as well as the above items, indicate the need for internal auditing to be involved in the development process, communication process, and attestation process related to publications and training programs.

Common Practices

In prior studies, organizations have identified a variety of methods used to communicate compliance policies and procedures. These include publications such as codes of conduct, policy manuals, brochures, in-house newspapers, and fact sheets. Training programs include orientation sessions, interactive video training, periodic seminars, staff meetings, and videotaped messages from the CEO. In most organizations, more than one method is used.

Organizations often develop communication systems that fit their environment. For example, one large company uses a software program called Lawyer in a Laptop to provide assistance to sales representatives dealing with difficult legal compliance issues. The concept is based on the assumption that more learning takes place through actual practice than in the classroom. Other organizations are likely to develop their own unique methods of communicating compliance policies.

Codes of Conduct

One of the most common methods of meeting this requirement of the Guidelines is the use of a Code of Conduct or Code of Ethics. Respondents to the 1994 Defense Industry Initiative survey stated that most of their codes address issues including kickbacks, conflicts of interest, confidential information, and business courtesies.[2]

Business Considerations — A Checklist for Codes of Conduct

Q1. Does your company have a code of ethics or standards of conduct?

A. Although the official name for the document may vary, this is basically a "Yes" or "No" response.

Q2. What are the implications of adopting a code of ethics?

A. Organizations that adopt a code of ethics raise their employee's expectations; expectations that can quickly turn into cynicism unless top managers practice what they preach. They are explicitly telling their employees the company's specific areas of concern. Having a code that managers disregard is arguably worse than having no code at all. With disregarded codes, employees believe that ethical lapses are purposeful and not an oversight.

B. A code can also be a document that improves morale and creates employee empowerment to withstand temptations. Employees may view the code development and implementation process as a rallying point which either memorializes the company's commitment to ethics, or points to a new direction. Codes can empower employees who feel unable to challenge their immediate supervisor's questionable directives. If these directives now contradict an explicit policy within the code, lower level employees can discuss the order by pointing out the code discrepancy to the supervisor.[3]

Q3. Who will be involved in the code development process?

A. The code belongs to all employees and should be distributed to all employees, so arguably it should be constructed by a cross-section of all employees. Without a broad level of participation, groups that feel left out of the process will not "buy-in," or worse, may act to undermine the code. Without this broad level of acceptance, codes are expensive documents that neither satisfy corporate goals, nor qualify for fine reductions.

B. Internal auditors can play an important role in the code development process for several reasons. Auditors take a broader view of the entire company than many other departments. They are also skilled at operationalizing the outside legal and regulatory environment into corporate practice. Because compliance with many of these same laws and regulations will be addressed within the code, it is a natural progression to utilize the internal auditor's skills in the code development process.

Q4. What areas should be addressed within the code of conduct?

A. A Code of Ethics task force should determine what are the areas of risk and the necessary policies and procedures for the organization to minimize the exposure from these risks.

B. Management should provide employees with an opportunity to express their concerns and provide input as to what they would like addressed within the code. This can be accomplished with: (1) employee surveys, (2) focus groups (either cross-disciplinary or functional area specific), (3) personal interviews, or a combination of all three.

C. After input has been obtained, the process of developing a code is difficult to stop without negative ramifications. Following widespread surveys and interviews, employees will begin to expect the end product — the Code of Ethics. Failure to produce can once again breed cynicism.

[2]For further information, contact the DII at 1299 Pennsylvania Avenue, NW, 4th Floor, Washington, DC 20004.

[3]See Sears' Code of Business Conduct in Appendix C for an example of a code which provides broad guidance, but also presents specific fact situations and gives concrete answers.

D. After the internal risk analysis and employee survey, a policy review should be conducted. Are policies in place which will address all of the concerns? If not, can new ones be developed to address these risks?

Q5. After the information has been collected and analyzed, what will be the "tone" of the code?

A. Codes of ethics range from the harsh "Thou shalt not" attorney drafted codes, to values laden, ambiguous statements about core values. Neither one is "best" for all companies. Some companies are heavily regulated and use the codes as an additional opportunity to instruct their employees about the importance of complying with the regulations. Others believe that it is more important to express core values, from which employees should be able to interpret the "right way" to handle difficult situations.[4]

Q6. Should employees sign an annual certification that they have read the code and agree to abide by its policies?

A. Annual certification can accomplish several goals. Theoretically it can serve as a time for all employees to reflect upon the company's commitment to ethics and renew their personal commitment to the company's core values. It can also serve as a useful record that employees acknowledge having a copy of the code, without any knowledge of violations. This record may prove useful during future prosecution or litigation.

B. Unfortunately the annual signing ritual is sometimes treated lightly by employees. Some supervisors require their subordinates to certify that they understand the code even before the employee has had a chance to read the code. Some employees who have never witnessed a violation may roll their eyes and think to themselves, "Yes, I swear I have been ethical for another year." Employees who have intentionally committed violations will undoubtedly lie about it during certification. Some employees may have witnessed questionable activities, but are unwilling to get involved, fearing it will impact their careers. These employees will convince themselves that they are better off just checking the box stating that they have not witnessed any violations. One group, those who have witnessed questionable acts and are struggling with how to address them, may provide useful information. For these employees, certification can serve as the moment of truth. Should they: (1) divulge the information, (2) lie on a signed statement that they have no knowledge of misdeeds, or (3) refuse to sign the statement? This group of employees may come forward with their concerns rather than lie on the certification.

[4]Sears distributes a folder of information titled "Freedoms and Obligations" to all of its managers. Included within this package are three distinct, yet integrated parts: (1) the section on shared beliefs, (2) Leadership Principles, and (3) the Code of Business Conduct. The "tone" of the package is more inspirational than rigidly regulatory.

CHAPTER 9
REQUIREMENT #5

"The organization must have taken reasonable steps to achieve compliance with its standards, e.g., by utilizing monitoring and auditing systems reasonably designed to detect criminal conduct by its employees and other agents and by having in place and publicizing a reporting system whereby employees and other agents could report criminal conduct by others within the organization without fear of retribution." — (FSG#5)

Introduction

This is the requirement that directly impacts internal auditors. The first part of the requirement requires an organization to monitor its compliance systems, an activity most likely performed by the internal auditing function. The latter part of the requirement describes the need for a system where employees can report wrongdoings. The traditional reporting mechanism of problems within organizations is for employees to discuss their concerns with their immediate supervisor. Even though this is the appropriate method for handling most problems, there are occasions when employees need additional reporting mechanisms (ARMs).

Survey Results

Based on the survey, internal auditors and compliance officers generally consider their current status on this requirement to be good. On a 5-point scale, with 5 indicating a very high rating of current compliance with the requirement, internal auditor responses resulted in a mean score of 3.55, while compliance officers report a mean of 3.7. This rating was the second lowest mean score given by the compliance officers and the third lowest by internal auditors. The frequency of responses, as shown in Figure 9-1, illustrates that although few respondents gave their program a below average score, many were reluctant to rate the program as very good.

Figure 9-1
Assessment of Compliance with FSG#5
(Percentage of Respondents by Group)

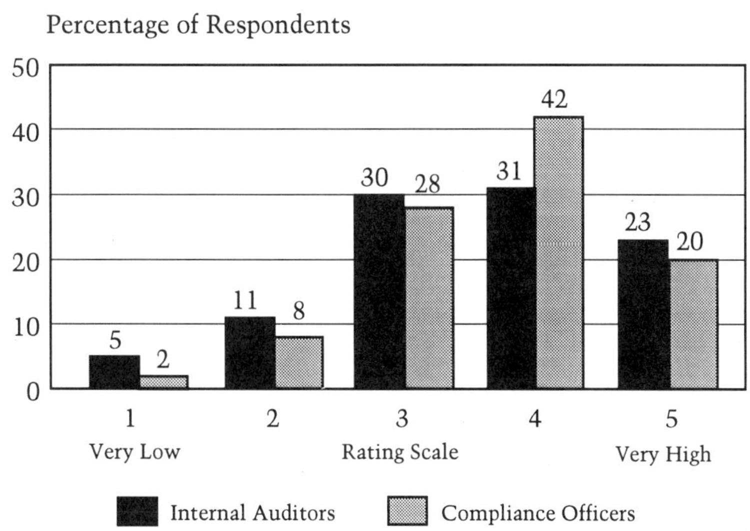

Role of the Internal Auditor

The role of the internal auditor regarding this requirement, as with other requirements, varies considerably. Based on our interviews, internal auditors may be involved in activities related to the design, monitoring, and investigation of reported failures. Figure 9-2 displays the frequency distribution of responses related to internal auditor activities. Considering as significant reported values of "4" or "5" (5-point scale with "5" indicating "very involved"), 50% of respondents reported significant involvement in design activities, 63% reported significant involvement in monitoring activities, and 73% reported significant involvement in activities related to the investigation of reported failures. These percentages are higher than the percentages of activities related to other FSG requirements. The higher percentages indicate that internal auditing is more involved with FSG#5.

When compliance programs have been imposed on organizations by the courts, a common condition is to require an annual audit of the organization's compliance program by an independent auditor. Internal auditors who report directly to the board of directors may be considered independent.

The increased need for services from internal auditors can be accomplished by internal auditing with: (1) expanded procedures within current auditing activities, and (2) a special audit of the organization's formal compliance program. Regarding expanded procedures, internal auditors often use risk assessment to determine areas upon which to focus. High risk compliance issues should be a part of that risk assessment. Within current internal auditing activities, specifically when there is an assessment of controls, the requirements of the Federal Sentencing Guidelines should also be considered.

Many internal auditing departments are now auditing the organization's formal compliance program. They are evaluating the effectiveness of the design of the program as well as monitoring the program and investigating reported failures. To qualify for fine reductions, the compliance program that was designed must be operating effectively. The annual reports by internal auditing regarding the compliance program would provide valuable documentation for the system.

Figure 9-2
Internal Audit Involvement with Design, Monitoring, and Investigation Activities (FSG#5)

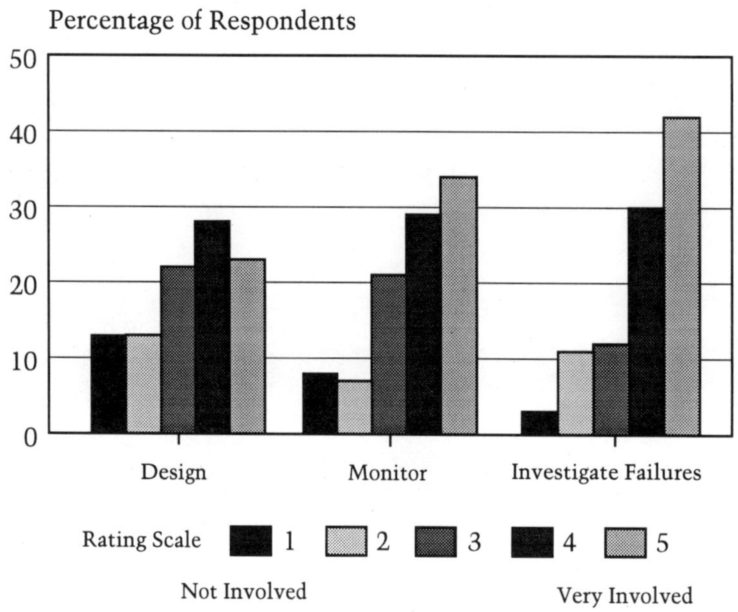

Figure 9-3
Additional Reporting Mechanisms

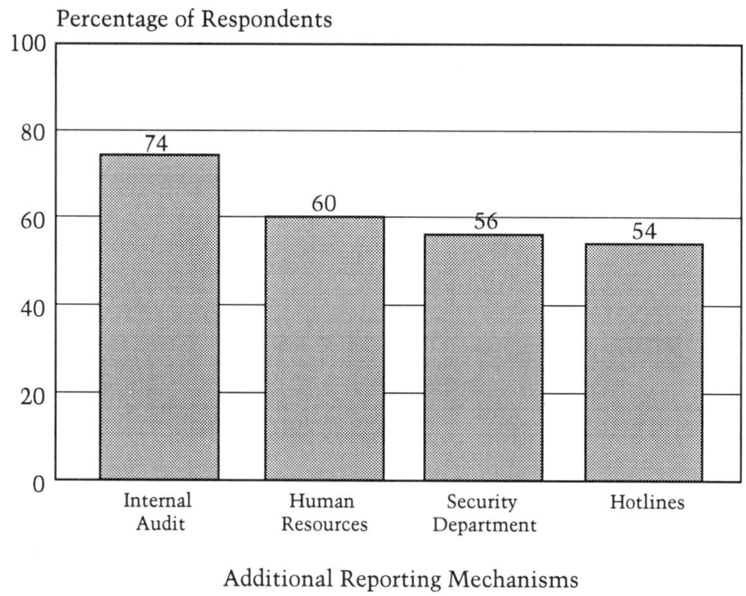

Common Practices

The survey asked respondents to identify the reporting mechanisms, other than reporting to the supervisor, that would be available to employees to report suspected wrongdoings. As shown in Figure 9-3, the most common response was "report to internal audit." Other frequent responses included: reporting to human resources, reporting to the security department, and reporting to hotlines. Most organizations had multiple options available for reporting wrongdoing.

When asked to provide highly effective or unique practices, hotlines were the most common response. Other items that were noted include: security department reports to internal auditing, internal auditing reports directly to the audit committee, and written requests to employees to bring concerns to the general auditor.

Additional Reporting Mechanisms (ARMs)

In this chapter, instead of a business considerations checklist, a detailed discussion of additional reporting mechanisms is presented.

There are occasions when employees need mechanisms other than the chain of command, i.e., additional reporting mechanisms (ARMs). The most common form of an ARM is the hotline. Yet, as discussed earlier, the additional reporting mechanism may also be channeled through a department such as internal auditing, security, or human resources. Management's challenge is to provide an additional reporting mechanism in which employees feel comfortable reporting their concerns. Without this type of mechanism, employees will either let concerns fester until they become deadened to their surrounding problems, leave the company, or report to an outside agency or news organization.

Each of these actions represents a failure on management's part. Proactive managers want information about potential problem areas before they explode. The challenge for management is in constructing an additional reporting mechanism that engenders enough trust to encourage employees to come forward with their concerns.

The mechanism for receiving the information, what is done with the information, and what happens to the reporter after the recommendation, will either foster or destroy the environment of trust. Employees will only use additional reporting mechanisms when they believe that companies will deal with their message and not kill the messenger. The factors that will instill this trust are: (1) confidentiality, (2) fairness, and (3) thoroughness.

Confidentiality

The person using the additional reporting mechanism (referred to as the "reporter") must believe that his or her career will not be affected by telling the truth. Anonymity in the process will help this perception. Many defense contractors have formalized their procedure for protecting the informant's identity. These companies use various administrative approaches to ensure confidentiality of hotline communications. Case numbers and code words for identification may be assigned to preserve the anonymity of the caller as an investigation is conducted. Companies explicitly restrict access to reports, documentation, and results of investigations to those with a legitimate need to know. Answering machines for recorded messages are locked away and records carefully safeguarded.

Some organizations go to great lengths to ensure that an informant's identity is not inadvertently revealed if permission is not given. For example, in the absence of the informant's consent to reveal his or her identity, one company requires the ombudsman to edit all information received through the ethics hotline to protect the informant's identity, even before the ombudsman assigns the investigation to another individual. The edit is extensive and includes, among other changes, replacing personal pronouns with the term "informant," removing information that provides specific details about the office or unit of the informant, transcribing any of the informant's handwritten correspondence, stamping "company sensitive" on all correspondence referred for examination, and, if appropriate, indicating on the material that it is subject to the attorney-client privilege. Furthermore, if an investigation cannot proceed without the informant's identity being revealed overtly, the company mandates that the informant be so advised, and, in determining whether or not to pursue an investigation, the ombudsman must take into consideration concerns about the disclosure of the informant's identity.

One problem with anonymity is that it makes feedback to the reporter more difficult. While some companies do not give feedback when anonymity is involved, others have developed procedures to satisfy even anonymous callers. With feedback, reporters have a sense of closure and accomplishment. Without feedback, they will not know the status of the investigation and may get discouraged.

The same concern for the reporter's rights will protect the violator and limit the amount of information available for feedback. Even if a violator is reprimanded, reporters may never know about the action unless they actually see the offender terminated or transferred. Organizations must balance the reporter's need for feedback with the accused's need for privacy.

Fairness

Investigators (ombudsmen, ethics coordinators, compliance officers, security officers, internal auditors, or in-house attorneys) must avoid the appearance that they are "out to get" the employees. If employees believe that these people and processes keep them from doing their jobs effectively, anyone suspected of becoming an informant will be shunned by their peers. Whoever handles the investigation must convince everyone involved that it will be conducted fairly.

Fairness requires respect for both the rights of the accuser and the accused. The accused must believe that investigators will only act on legitimate complaints, not secondhand gossip. This is appropriate because of the potentially devastating impact on the careers of those investigated. Even people cleared of any wrongdoings often carry the stigma that, "Maybe we did not catch you this time, but we will be watching you in the future."

Protecting the reporter's identity is very important, except in cases where the investigator believes the reporter is maliciously falsifying a complaint to damage someone's reputation. This is the only situation in which it is important to investigate and reprimand the reporter.

Thoroughness

The reporter must believe that the investigator will listen to every substantiated complaint with an open mind. The investigator must conduct a timely, aggressive, and complete inquiry into the allegation. After the review, investigators should make recommendations and report their findings to the audit committee of the board, CEO of the company, division manager, or an offender's immediate supervisor. The suggestions should include possible sanctions against problem employees, plus methods to remedy problem processes.

CHAPTER 10
REQUIREMENT #6

"The standards must have been consistently enforced through appropriate disciplinary mechanism, including, as appropriate, discipline of individuals responsible for the failure to detect an offense. Adequate discipline of individuals responsible for an offense is a necessary component of enforcement; however, the form of discipline that will be appropriate will be case specific." — (FSG#6)

Introduction

The discussion of the first five requirements of the Guidelines, Chapters 5 through 9, describes proactive policies and procedures to prevent and detect violations. FSG#6 and FSG#7 are reactive and discuss the minimum steps to take after violations have occurred. FSG#6 calls for consistent discipline, including discipline for the person who failed to detect the violation. FSG#7, discussed in Chapter 11, states that the organization must "respond appropriately," and describe its process modifications in enough detail to convince the judge that this type of violation should not occur in the future.

While intuition tells us that employers should administer consistent discipline for similar violations, organizations sometimes act counter-intuitively. Different managers may determine different punishments for similar offenders. Also, factors like favoritism, nepotism, and star performance can cloud a manager's decision making about punishing violations. Unfortunately, when this happens organizations send the implicit message that violations are only considered offenses if violators are in a non-privileged group. Employees will not strive to minimize their violations, rather they will try to maximize their status within the organization so they can be immune from punishment. Employee morale will ratchet ever lower as they watch the company administer a multi-tier system of justice, one for the "haves" and others for everyone else.

The second requirement of the section is to discipline supervisors who failed to detect violations which occurred under their watch. Organizations should hold their supervisors to the same standard they are held to under the Guidelines — due diligence, not perfection. Supervisors who faithfully administer the organization's compliance programs should not be punished because a rogue employee or problem process turned up in their department.

Survey Results

Based on survey results, internal auditors and compliance officers generally consider their current status on this requirement to be good. Using a 5-point scale, with 5 indicating a very high rating of current compliance with the requirement, internal auditor responses resulted in a mean score of 3.32, while compliance officers reported a mean of 3.38. Yet, these means were the lowest of all the ratings for the seven requirements. The frequency of responses, as shown in Figure 10-1, reveals that over 40% of both internal auditors and compliance officers rated their programs in the middle of the scale, with about 30% of each group willing to give it a higher than average, but not "very high," rating. This indicates that FSG#6 could be the requirement needing the most attention in many organizations.

Figure 10-1
Assessment of Compliance with FSG#6
(Percentage of Responses by Group)

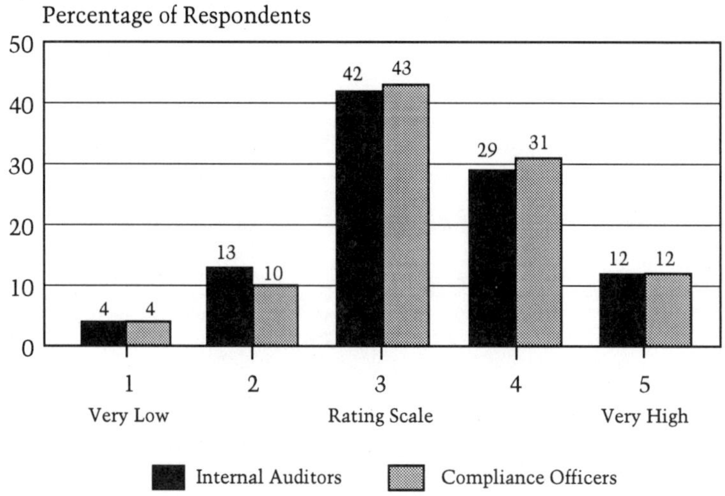

FSG#6: "The standards must have been consistently enforced through appropriate disciplinary mechanism, including, as appropriate, discipline of individuals responsible for the failure to detect an offense. Adequate discipline of individuals responsible for an offense is a necessary component of enforcement; however, the form of discipline that will be appropriate will be case specific."

Role of the Internal Auditor

The respondents indicated that the human resources and legal departments are the groups most involved with consistent discipline. As shown in Figure 10-2, 51% of the respondents indicated the involvement of these two functional areas. Internal auditors were identified as being responsible

Figure 10-2
Groups Identified as Responsible for
Consistent Discipline

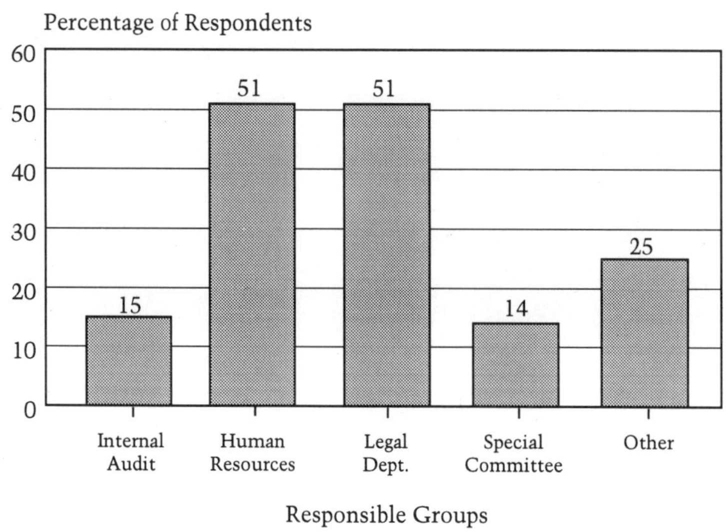

Figure 10-3
Internal Audit's Role in Consistent Discipline

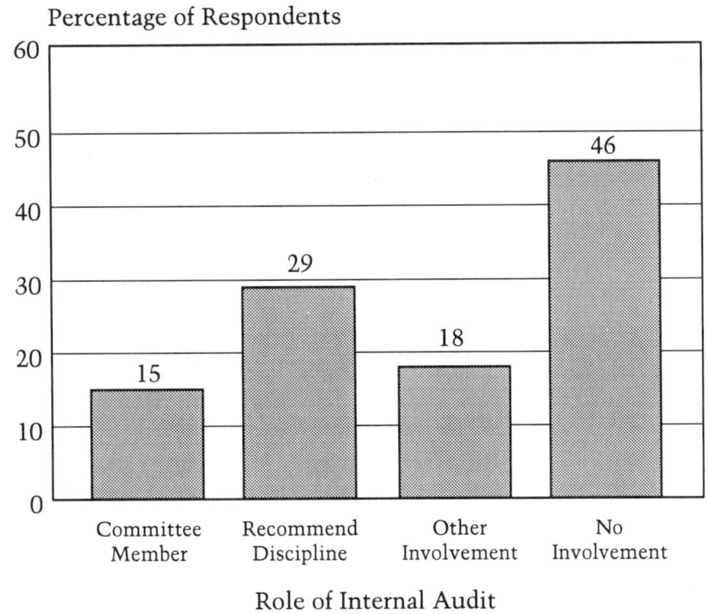

for consistent discipline by 15% of the respondents. Regardless of who is responsible for consistent discipline, others may be involved in the process. A separate question asked respondents to identify any involvement of internal auditing related to consistent discipline. As shown in Figure 10-3, 46% of the respondents indicated no involvement, while 29% indicated that internal auditing makes recommendations for disciplinary action to the committee, and 15% indicated that internal auditors were members of the committee.

Business Considerations

The final section of this chapter presents a list of questions to assist in the evaluation of FSG#6 for your organization.

Q1. Has your organization communicated understandable policies about what constitutes a violation and their corresponding disciplinary response?

A. It is not enough to have policies detailing violations. These policies must be understandable by the group they are intended to cover. The policies should also be communicated in a handbook, Code of Ethics, and employee training to reinforce their importance.

Q2. Are disciplinary actions reported to a central location that reviews for consistency?

A. Without a reviewing mechanism, discipline tends to be situational rather than universal. The company risks sending conflicting messages if violations are tolerated in one division, but strictly enforced in another.

Q3. Are supervisors evaluated on their compliance efforts as part of their performance review?

A. Some people will only pay attention to an initiative like compliance if it is considered a part of their evaluation. By including it in the evaluation, companies are reinforcing the importance of compliance. Inclusion also allows managers who do a particularly good or bad job to be either rewarded or punished for their efforts.

CHAPTER 11
REQUIREMENT #7

"After an offense has been detected, the organization must have taken all reasonable steps to respond appropriately to the offense and to prevent further similar offenses — Including any necessary modifications to its program to prevent and detect violations of law." — (FSG#7)

Introduction

What is an appropriate response by the organization after it has detected that a violation has occurred? First, the company should conduct a thorough and expedient investigation. It is important to document all the steps involved during the investigation and corrective action taken after the investigation.

A critical issue is to determine whether, what, and when information about potential violations will be reported to the government. Some organizations have a close working relationship with governmental authorities and contact them immediately once a potential problem surfaces. These companies then conduct a thorough investigation, take corrective action, and give a full report to the appropriate government authority.

Survey Results

Based on survey results, internal auditors and compliance officers generally consider their current status on this requirement to be very good. Using a 5-point scale, with 5 indicating a very high rating of current compliance with the requirement, internal auditor responses resulted in a mean score of 3.7, while compliance officers reported a mean of 3.71. These mean responses were almost the

Figure 11-1
Assessment of Compliance with FSG#7
(Percentage of Responses by Group)

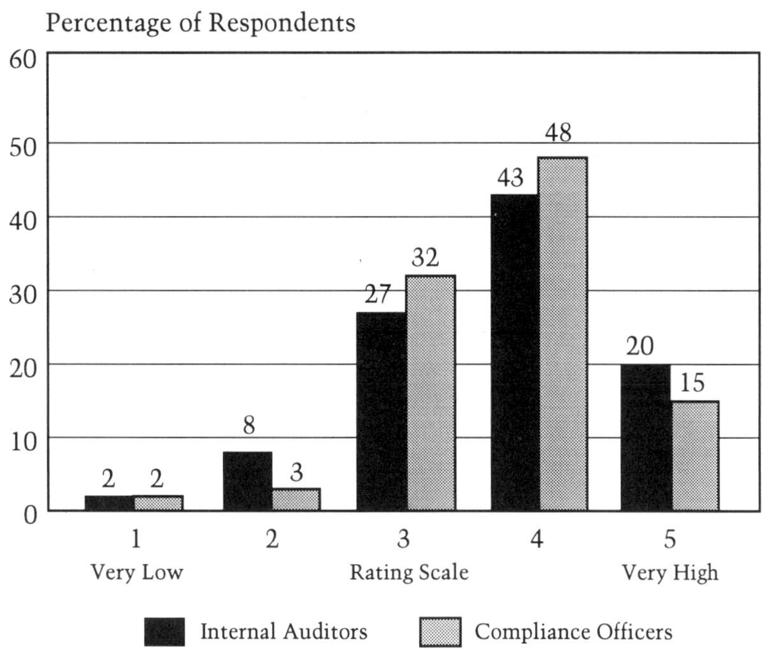

same for the two groups of respondents. The frequency of responses, as shown in Figure 11-1, reveals that more than 40% of both internal auditors and compliance officers rated their programs in the high category (rating of 4 on a 5 point scale). Very few respondents from both groups gave a low rating to this item.

Role of the Internal Auditor

The role of the internal auditor regarding this requirement, as with other requirements, varies considerably. Based on our interviews, internal auditors may be involved in activities related to the design and the evaluation process. Figure 11-2 displays the frequency distribution of responses related to internal auditor activities. Considering reported values of "4" or "5" as significant (5-point scale with "5" indicating "very involved"), 54% of respondents reported significant involvement in design activities and 66% reported significant involvement in activities related to the evaluation of changes necessary to prevent further similar offenses.

Figure 11-2
Internal Audit Involvement with Design and Evaluation Activities (FSG#7)

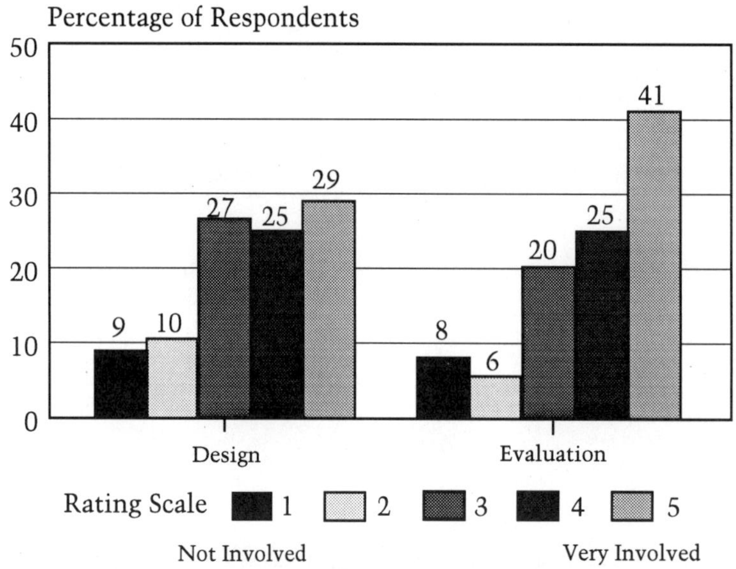

Business Considerations

The final section of this chapter presents a list of questions to assist in the evaluation of FSG#7 for the organization.

Q1. What does the organization do after potential problems are detected?

A. To qualify for fine reductions, companies should conduct an immediate investigation of the potential problem. Organizations must identify the root cause of the violation. Once detected, corrective action should be taken and the process should be modified to minimize the risk of a repeat offense.

Q2. What internal controls were in place to detect the root cause of the violation?

A. Once the internal control has been identified, it must be evaluated to determine its adequacy. No internal control will prevent every violation, but can this control be modified to detect and prevent similar violations in the future?

CHAPTER 12 VOLUNTARY DISCLOSURE VERSUS PRIVILEGE

The preceding chapters analyzed the requirements of establishing an effective compliance program that prevents and detects violations. This chapter examines the value of voluntary disclosure and whether third parties can use the disclosed information against them in subsequent civil litigation. Some organizations believe that they are better off not having any compliance programs at all. Even if they have a compliance program, it is argued that the results of internal investigations should not be voluntarily disclosed to the government. The rationale for these arguments is that the company should make obtaining evidence as difficult as possible for government investigators and any subsequent third-party plaintiffs.

Voluntary Disclosure

Two questions arise when considering voluntary disclosure. The first is, will an organization lose all of its privilege arguments regarding information which is voluntarily disclosed to the government? The second question deals with how organizations are treated by the government after voluntary disclosure. To encourage self-reporting, these disclosing organizations should be treated better than those who are uncooperative. Absent favorable governmental treatment, organizations will be sent the message that it makes more sense to seek fine reductions by developing an effective compliance program, but not pursue the additional reductions for self-disclosure.

There are additional benefits to conducting a thorough internal investigation and reporting the results to the appropriate governmental authority. A proactive investigation may prevent or limit the scope of a government investigation. If the organization discloses the violation to the government, the company may be able to convince the appropriate agency not to criminally indict, but instead use available civil and administrative remedies.

The preceding chapters have discussed the advantages of compliance programs and voluntary disclosure, but every company will have to conduct its own cost-benefit analysis. The Guidelines reward compliant corporations with fine reductions. The Guidelines give an even greater reward to those that both comply and voluntarily disclose. The best case scenario would have organizations comply, disclose, and then be protected by privilege against subsequent civil lawsuits.

Privilege

Even though the concept of privilege is in a state of flux without guaranteed protection, organizations can take steps that will maximize the probability of successfully asserting privilege as a defense. This chapter analyzes the concepts of: (1) attorney-client privilege, (2) work-product privilege, (3) self-evaluative privilege, and (4) waiver, and lists suggestions to help secure their use.

Attorney-Client Privilege

The attorney-client privilege protects confidential communications between client and attorney for the purpose of securing legal advice. This definition contains several parts: (1) communication between attorney and client, (2) confidentiality, and (3) for the purpose of obtaining legal advice.

In order to be privileged the communication must be between client and attorney. When dealing with corporations and in-house or outside counsel, one question becomes apparent, "Who is the client?" Typically the attorney has been hired by the company and is supposed to represent its best interests. Communications between lower-level employees and the attorney may not be privileged because they are not considered to be the client.

Regarding confidentiality, what efforts have the attorney and the client made to treat this information as private? It is advisable to stamp the communications as "Private," or "Confidential," or "Subject to the Attorney-Client Privilege." While stamping documents does not guarantee that the courts will treat them as privileged, failing to stamp them will increase the likelihood that courts will not consider them privileged. Once these documents have been stamped, they should only be distributed to those with a need to know. Widespread distribution will provide a strong argument against confidentiality.

The last requirement deals with communications to secure legal advice. Even though the communication is issued by an attorney, this privilege will not attach if the attorney is issuing business advice. Sometimes the line between legal and business advice can seem blurred. Because this falls into a "gray area," it is important that clients specifically request their attorney to provide legal advice.

Work-Product Privilege

This privilege deals with information and investigations conducted by an attorney in anticipation of litigation. One of the greatest weaknesses of the work-product privilege is the "anticipation of litigation" requirement. This means that routine practices will not necessarily be privileged. Just as with the attorney-client privilege, documents prepared for business purposes will not be protected.

Self-Evaluative Privilege

The "self-evaluative privilege," or "self-critical analysis," represents organizations' most recent attempt to protect information. This privilege is designed to allow organizations to aggressively investigate violations without fear of creating a road map for subsequent third-party lawsuits. There is a three-prong test to satisfy the self-evaluative privilege: (1) there must be an internal critique, (2) the evaluation should be encouraged as a matter of public policy, and (3) disclosure of the evaluation would discourage future self-critical analysis. Judges will weigh the public policy behind encouraging this self-evaluative privilege against the plaintiff's needs for the information.

There are several advantages of the self-evaluative privilege over attorney-client, or the work-product privilege. These advantages include: (1) the fact that they do not have to be conducted by or for an attorney, (2) the reviews may be privileged even if there is no anticipation of litigation, and (3) it allows the organization to critically evaluate its compliance programs. One of the major disadvantages is that this privilege is not as well established and has not been widely adopted by the courts.

Waiver

Organizations risk waiving any of the privileges by voluntarily disclosing information. This places the company in the unenviable position of wanting to qualify for the maximum fine reductions measured against the fear of having that information used against them in subsequent civil litigation.

Conclusion

In order to encourage good citizenship through voluntary disclosure, some states and federal agencies are providing additional statutory protections. The authors would call on federal and state legislators to expand the self-evaluative privilege to allow this type of self-critical analysis without fearing its subsequent use. The expansion of this privilege will promote the free flow of information to regulators and benefit the public in the long run.

CHAPTER 13
CONCLUSION

Because the Federal Sentencing Guidelines are being used as a benchmark, internal auditors should become very familiar with the identified seven minimum requirements for an effective compliance program. Internal auditors can play an important role in implementing the Guidelines. They understand the regulatory environment and are experts in operationalizing plans which satisfy these regulations. Internal auditors should be actively involved in maintaining effective proactive compliance programs as part of a strong system of controls.

The preceding chapters have presented an overview of the Guidelines and the impact they have on the profession of internal auditing. While the Guidelines provide an excellent starting point, there is no "compliance program in a box" or "one program fits all" scenario. The Guidelines will place different demands upon different organizations depending upon company size, inherent risks within a given industry, and how similarly placed companies are addressing these risks. Organizations must reflect upon their particular strengths and weaknesses and then develop compliance programs to prevent and detect possible violations.

While it is necessary to recognize the potential impact of the Guidelines and dedicate resources to implement compliance programs, this may not be sufficient. There are no quick fixes. The most effective compliance programs will be developed when managers and employees develop a "Partnership of Trust" in stopping violations. This partnership begins to develop when managers give employees the necessary resources to perform their jobs in an ethical fashion. Another important component of engendering trust requires that employees who report violations should never fear retaliation. The organization will be the ultimate beneficiary of this "Partnership" by creating a work environment that simultaneously decreases the potential of violations and improves morale.

BIBLIOGRAPHY

Books:

The Business Roundtable, *Corporate Ethics: A Prime Business Asset,* (1988).

Committee of Sponsoring Organizations of the Treadway Commission (COSO), (1992) *Internal Control - Integrated Framework.*

Defense Industry Initiative on Business Ethics and Conduct, *1993 Annual Report to the Public and the Defense Industry* (1994).

Kaplan, J. M. , J. E. Murphy, and W. M. Swenson, *Compliance Programs and the Corporate Sentencing Guidelines* (Deerfield, IL: Clark, Boardman, and Callaghan, 1995).

Rakoff, J. S., L. R. Blumkin, and R. A. Sauber, *Corporate Sentencing Guidelines: Compliance and Litigation* (Law Journal Seminars-Press: New York, 1994).

The Ethics Resource Center and The Behavior Research Center, *Ethics Policies and Programs in American Business,* (Washington, D.C.: Ethics Resource Center and the Behavior Research Center, 1990).

United States Sentencing Commission, *Annual Report,* (Washington, D.C.: United States Sentencing Commission, 1993).

United States Sentencing Commission, *Corporate Crime in America: Strengthening the "Good Citizen" Corporation,* (Washington, D.C.: United States Sentencing Commission, 1995).

Articles:

Fiorelli, Paul E., "Fine Reductions Through Effective Ethics Programs," *Albany Law Review,* Vol. 56, No. 2 (1992).

Fiorelli, Paul E., "Guideline Amendments Dramatically Change the Structure of Organizational Fines," *The Catholic Lawyer,* Vol. 35, No. 2 (1993).

Fiorelli, Paul E. and Rooney, Cynthia J., "The Environmental Sentencing Guidelines For Business Organizations: Are There Murky Waters in Their Future?" *Boston College Environmental Affairs Law Review,* Vol. 22 (1994).

Jordan, Kirk S., "Lesson in Organizational Compliance: A Survey of Government Imposed Compliance Programs," *Corporate Counsel's Quarterly,* Vol. 11, No. 4 (1995).

Rovella, David E., "Laws May Ease the Risky Business of Job References," *National Law Journal,* October 23, 1995 at B-2.

Smallhouse, Mark K., "Intel's *Lawyer in a Laptop:* Re-Defining Corporate Compliance Training Programs," *Preventive Law Reporter,* Vol. 13, No. 4 (Winter 1994).

Truell, Peter, "Daiwa Bank Admits Guilt in Cover-Up," *The New York Times,* February 29, 1996.

APPENDIX A
QUESTIONNAIRES

Questionnaire for Internal Auditors Regarding the Federal Sentencing Guidelines

The following questions are designed to consider the impact of the Federal Sentencing Guidelines on your organization. ***All responses will be confidential.*** Questionnaires are coded to match the two responses from each organization. To ensure confidentiality, no record was made regarding which questionnaire number was sent to any individual organization. We greatly appreciate your assistance.

Section I — Overview

1. How familiar are you with the Federal Sentencing Guidelines as they affect organizations?

EXTREMELY FAMILIAR				NOT FAMILIAR
5	4	3	2	1

2. What is your perception of the impact of the Sentencing Guidelines on your organization?

SIGNIFICANT IMPACT				NO IMPACT
5	4	3	2	1

   a. Why do you believe the Sentencing Guidelines will have the impact you described? (Select all that apply.)
   ___ Federal, state, or industry regulations already satisfy the requirements.
   ___ Industry has few potential violations.
   ___ Size of the organization.
   ___ Sophistication of current systems.
   ___ Analysis by legal department.
   ___ Other, please specify ______________________

3. Indicate which statement most accurately reflects the involvement of Internal Audit in your organization's overall "compliance program."
   ___ No compliance program in place, therefore no involvement.
   ___ Compliance program is separate from Internal Audit, no involvement.
   ___ Key members of Internal Audit are members of a compliance committee.
   ___ Internal Audit is the compliance program.
   ___ Other, please specify ______________________

4. Estimate the percentage of the Internal Audit department's time spent in the following types of audit activities.
   ___ % Operational
   ___ % Financial
   ___ % Compliance
   ___ % Other, please specify ______________________
   100%

Section II — Seven Minimum Requirements

The 7 minimum requirements of an effective compliance program as identified by the Federal Sentencing Guidelines are listed below. After each item is a series of questions related to Internal Audit's involvement.

1. ***"The organization must have established compliance standards and procedures to be followed by its employees and other agents that are reasonably capable of reducing the prospect of criminal conduct."***

   a. Overall, how would you rate your organization's current compliance with the item listed above?

VERY HIGH	ABOVE AVERAGE	AVERAGE	BELOW AVERAGE	VERY LOW
5	4	3	2	1

   b. How involved is your Internal Audit department in the **design, monitoring, and investigation of reported failures** of these standards and procedures?

	VERY INVOLVED				NOT INVOLVED
Design	5	4	3	2	1
Monitoring	5	4	3	2	1
Investigation of reported failures	5	4	3	2	1

   c. Please share with us any policies and procedures related to requirement #1 which you believe to be highly effective or unique.

2. ***"Specific individual(s) within high-level personnel of the organization must have been assigned overall responsibility to oversee compliance with such standards and procedures."***

a. Overall, how would you rate your organization's current compliance with the item listed above?

VERY HIGH	ABOVE AVERAGE	AVERAGE	BELOW AVERAGE	VERY LOW
5	4	3	2	1

b. Which of the following best describes your organization's person or committee responsible for this function?

___ An Individual
  ___ Compliance officer
  ___ Ethics officer
  ___ Ombudsman
  ___ An individual in legal
  ___ An individual in auditing
  ___ An individual in human resources
  ___ Other, please specify ____________
___ A Committee
  ___ A standing committee of top management.
  ___ A special committee designated only for this purpose.
  ___ Other, please specify ____________

c. How is the Internal Audit department involved in the oversight of the compliance program?

___ Involved as members of the oversight committee.
___ Involved in the selection of the individual who is in charge of compliance.
___ Other involvement, please specify. ________
___ Not involved.

d. Please share with us any policies and procedures related to requirement #2 which you believe to be highly effective or unique.

3. ***"The organization must have used due care not to delegate substantial discretionary authority to individuals whom the organization knew, or should have known through the exercise of due diligence, had a propensity to engage in illegal activities."***

a. Overall, how would you rate your organization's current compliance with the item listed above?

VERY HIGH	ABOVE AVERAGE	AVERAGE	BELOW AVERAGE	VERY LOW
5	4	3	2	1

b. How involved is your Internal Audit department in the **design, monitoring, and investigation of reported failures** of these standards and procedures?

	VERY INVOLVED				NOT INVOLVED
Design	5	4	3	2	1
Monitoring	5	4	3	2	1
Investigation of reported failures	5	4	3	2	1

c. Please share with us any policies and procedures related to requirement #3 which you believe to be highly effective or unique.

4. ***"The organization must have taken steps to communicate effectively its standards and procedures to all employees and other agents, e.g., by requiring participation in training programs or by disseminating publications that explain in a practical manner what is required."***

a. Overall, how would you rate your organization's current compliance with the item listed above?

VERY HIGH	ABOVE AVERAGE	AVERAGE	BELOW AVERAGE	VERY LOW
5	4	3	2	1

b. Internal Audit departments are sometimes involved with the following activities. Please indicate the involvement of your Internal Audit department in each of the following. (Omit any items that are not applicable.)

	VERY INVOLVED				NOT INVOLVED
Development of training programs or codes of conduct	5	4	3	2	1
Tracking any required internal certification of codes of conduct	5	4	3	2	1
Tracking participation in training programs	5	4	3	2	1
Contribution of "sanitized" actual cases for training purposes	5	4	3	2	1
Other, please specify ____________	5	4	3	2	1

c. Please share with us any policies and procedures related to requirement #4 which you believe to be highly effective or unique.

5. ***"The organization must have taken reasonable steps to achieve compliance with its standards, e.g., by utilizing monitoring and auditing systems reasonably designed to detect criminal conduct by its employees and other agents and by having in place and publicizing a reporting system whereby employees and other agents could report criminal conduct by others within the organization without fear of retribution."***

a. Overall, how would you rate your organization's current compliance with the item listed above?

VERY HIGH	ABOVE AVERAGE	AVERAGE	BELOW AVERAGE	VERY LOW
5	4	3	2	1

b. Often internal audit is responsible for the "monitoring and auditing systems reasonably designed to detect criminal conduct by its employees and other agents." How involved is your Internal Audit department in the **design, monitoring, and investigation of reported failures** of these systems?

	VERY INVOLVED				NOT INVOLVED
Design	5	4	3	2	1
Monitoring	5	4	3	2	1
Investigation of reported failures	5	4	3	2	1

c. How much impact has the COSO report had on the evaluation of internal controls in your organization?

SIGNIFICANT IMPACT				NO IMPACT
5	4	3	2	1

d. What types of reporting mechanisms, besides reporting concerns to their supervisor, are in place whereby employees can report suspected wrongdoings without fear of retribution?

___ Hotlines
___ Report to Internal Audit
___ Report to human resources
___ Report to security department
___ Other, please specify ____________________

e. Please share with us any policies or procedures related to requirement #5 which you believe to be highly effective or unique.

6. ***"The standards must have been consistently enforced through appropriate disciplinary mechanisms, including, as appropriate, discipline of individuals responsible for the failure to detect an offense. Adequate discipline of individuals responsible for an offense is a necessary component of enforcement; however, the form of discipline that will be appropriate will be case specific."***

a. Overall, how would you rate your organization's current compliance with the item listed above?

VERY HIGH	ABOVE AVERAGE	AVERAGE	BELOW AVERAGE	VERY LOW
5	4	3	2	1

b. Who is responsible for making sure that discipline is consistently enforced?

___ Human resources department
___ A special committee
___ Internal audit
___ Legal department
___ Other, please specify ____________________

c. How is the Internal Audit department involved in consistent enforcement of discipline?

___ Involved as members of a committee.
___ Involved in making recommendations for disciplinary action to the committee
___ Other involvement, please specify __________
___ Not involved

d. Please share with us any policies and procedures related to requirement #6 which you believe to be highly effective or unique.

7. ***"After an offense has been detected, the organization must have taken all reasonable steps to respond appropriately to the offense and to prevent further similar offenses — including any necessary modifications to its program to prevent and detect violations of law."***

a. Overall, how would you rate your organization's current compliance with the item listed above?

VERY HIGH	ABOVE AVERAGE	AVERAGE	BELOW AVERAGE	VERY LOW
5	4	3	2	1

b. How involved is your Internal Audit department in the **design and evaluation** of changes necessary to prevent further similar offenses?

	VERY INVOLVED				NOT INVOLVED
Design	5	4	3	2	1
Evaluation	5	4	3	2	1

c. Please share with us any policies and procedures related to requirement #7 which you believe to be highly effective or unique.

Section III — Demographics

Organizational Demographics

Primary Industry: ____________________

(or SIC code __________)

Other Industries: ____________________

(or SIC Codes ____________________)

Size of Organization:

Revenues ____________

Assets ____________

Number of Employees ________

Organizational Affiliations:

Business Roundtable ________

Defense Industry Initiative Signatory ______

Within your organization, were you able to identify an appropriate person to receive the additional questionnaire and forward the questionnaire to that individual?

Yes____

No ____

Individual Demographics

Job Title: ____________________

Number of years work experience in internal audit: ___

Number of years total work experience: ________

Professional Certifications: (circle all that apply)

CIA CMA CPA CBA Other ______

Professional Affiliations: (circle all that apply)

IIA FEI AICPA IMA Other ______

Gender: Male Female

Age: ______

Section IV — Final Comments

If you would be willing to further discuss the impact of the Federal Sentencing Guidelines on Internal Audit, please attach your business card. (To maintain questionnaire response confidentiality, business cards will be kept separately, or if you prefer, you may send your card in a different envelope.) If you have any questions regarding this questionnaire, please contact Paul E. Fiorelli at (513) 745-2050 or Cynthia J. Rooney at (513) 745-2011. We appreciate your assistance and welcome any additional comments you may have.

Questionnaire for Compliance/Ethics Officers Regarding the Federal Sentencing Guidelines

The following questions are designed to consider the impact of the Federal Sentencing Guidelines on your organization. ***All responses will be confidential.*** Questionnaires are coded to match the two responses from each organization. To ensure confidentiality, no record was made regarding which questionnaire number was sent to any individual organization. We greatly appreciate your assistance.

Section I — Overview

1. How familiar are you with the Federal Sentencing Guidelines as they affect organizations?

EXTREMELY FAMILIAR				NOT FAMILIAR
5	4	3	2	1

2. What is your perception of the impact of the Sentencing Guidelines on your organization?

SIGNIFICANT IMPACT				NO IMPACT
5	4	3	2	1

a. Why do you believe the Sentencing Guidelines will have the impact you described? (Select all that apply.)
- ___ Federal, state, or industry regulations already satisfy the requirements.
- ___ Industry has few potential violations.
- ___ Size of the organization.
- ___ Sophistication of current systems.
- ___ Analysis by legal department.
- ___ Other, please specify ______________________

Section II — Seven Minimum Requirements

The 7 minimum requirements of an effective compliance program as identified by the Federal Sentencing Guidelines are listed below. After each item is a series of questions related to Internal Audit's involvement.

1. ***"The organization must have established compliance standards and procedures to be followed by its employees and other agents that are reasonably capable of reducing the prospect of criminal conduct."***

a. Overall, how would you rate your organization's current compliance with the item listed above?

VERY HIGH	ABOVE AVERAGE	AVERAGE	BELOW AVERAGE	VERY LOW
5	4	3	2	1

b. Please share with us any policies and procedures related to requirement #1 which you believe to be highly effective or unique.

2. ***"Specific individual(s) within high-level personnel of the organization must have been assigned overall responsibility to oversee compliance with such standards and procedures."***

   a. Overall, how would you rate your organization's current compliance with the item listed above?

VERY HIGH	ABOVE AVERAGE	AVERAGE	BELOW AVERAGE	VERY LOW
5	4	3	2	1

   b. Which of the following best describes your organization's person or committee responsible for this function?
   ___ An Individual
      ___ Compliance officer
      ___ Ethics officer
      ___ Ombudsman
      ___ An individual in legal
      ___ An individual in auditing
      ___ An individual in human resources
      ___ Other, please specify ________________
   ___ A Committee
      ___ A standing committee of top management.
      ___ A special committee designated only for this purpose.
      ___ Other, please specify ________________

   c. How is the Internal Audit department involved in the oversight of the compliance program?
   ___ Involved as members of the oversight committee.
   ___ Involved in the selection of the individual who is in charge of compliance.
   ___ Other involvement, please specify. __________
   ___ Not involved.

   d. Please share with us any policies and procedures related to requirement #2 which you believe to be highly effective or unique.

3. ***"The organization must have used due care not to delegate substantial discretionary authority to individuals whom the organization knew, or should have known through the exercise of due diligence, had a propensity to engage in illegal activities."***

   a. Overall, how would you rate your organization's current compliance with the item listed above?

VERY HIGH	ABOVE AVERAGE	AVERAGE	BELOW AVERAGE	VERY LOW
5	4	3	2	1

   b. Please share with us any policies and procedures related to requirement #3 which you believe to be highly effective or unique.

4. ***"The organization must have taken steps to communicate effectively its standards and procedures to all employees and other agents, e.g., by requiring participation in training programs or by disseminating publications that explain in a practical manner what is required."***

a. Overall, how would you rate your organization's current compliance with the item listed above?

VERY HIGH	ABOVE AVERAGE	AVERAGE	BELOW AVERAGE	VERY LOW
5	4	3	2	1

b. Internal Audit departments are sometimes involved with the following activities. Please indicate the involvement of your Internal Audit department in each of the following. (Omit any items that are not applicable.)

	VERY INVOLVED				NOT INVOLVED
Development of training programs or codes of conduct	5	4	3	2	1
Tracking any required internal certification of codes of conduct	5	4	3	2	1
Tracking participation in training programs	5	4	3	2	1
Contribution of "sanitized" actual cases for training purposes	5	4	3	2	1
Other, please specify ________________	5	4	3	2	1

c. Please share with us any policies and procedures related to requirement #4 which you believe to be highly effective or unique.

5. ***"The organization must have taken reasonable steps to achieve compliance with its standards, e.g., by utilizing monitoring and auditing systems reasonably designed to detect criminal conduct by its employees and other agents and by having in place and publicizing a reporting system whereby employees and other agents could report criminal conduct by others within the organization without fear of retribution."***

a. Overall, how would you rate your organization's current compliance with the item listed above?

VERY HIGH	ABOVE AVERAGE	AVERAGE	BELOW AVERAGE	VERY LOW
5	4	3	2	1

b. Often internal audit is responsible for the "monitoring and auditing systems reasonably designed to detect criminal conduct by its employees and other agents." How involved is your Internal Audit department in the **design, monitoring, and investigation of reported failures** of these systems?

	VERY INVOLVED				NOT INVOLVED
Design	5	4	3	2	1
Monitoring	5	4	3	2	1
Investigation of reported failures	5	4	3	2	1

c. What types of reporting mechanisms, besides reporting concerns to their supervisor, are in place whereby employees can report suspected wrongdoings without fear of retribution?

___ Hotlines
___ Report to Internal Audit
___ Report to human resources
___ Report to security department
___ Other, please specify ________________

d. How are these additional reporting mechanisms communicated? (check all that apply.)

___ Codes of conduct
___ Training sessions
___ Phone directory
___ Posters
___ Other, please specify ________________

e. Please share with us any policies and procedures in requirement #5 which you believe to be highly effective or unique.

6. ***"The standards must have been consistently enforced through appropriate disciplinary mechanisms, including, as appropriate, discipline of individuals responsible for the failure to detect an offense. Adequate discipline of individuals responsible for an offense is a necessary component of enforcement; however, the form of discipline that will be appropriate will be case specific."***

   a. Overall, how would you rate your organization's current compliance with the item listed above?

VERY HIGH	ABOVE AVERAGE	AVERAGE	BELOW AVERAGE	VERY LOW
5	4	3	2	1

   b. Who is responsible for making sure that discipline is consistently enforced?
   ___ Human resources department
   ___ A special committee
   ___ Internal audit
   ___ Legal department
   ___ Other, please specify ____________________

   c. Please share with us any policies and procedures related to requirement #6 which you believe to be highly effective or unique.

7. ***"After an offense has been detected, the organization must have taken all reasonable steps to respond appropriately to the offense and to prevent further similar offenses — including any necessary modifications to its program to prevent and detect violations of law."***

   a. Overall, how would you rate your organization's current compliance with the item listed above?

VERY HIGH	ABOVE AVERAGE	AVERAGE	BELOW AVERAGE	VERY LOW
5	4	3	2	1

   b. Please share with us any policies and procedures related to requirement #7 which you believe to be highly effective or unique.

Section III — Demographics

Organizational Demographics

Primary Industry: SIC code ____________________
(or industry name ____________________)
Other Industries: SIC codes ____________________
(or industry names ____________________)
Size of Organization:
Revenues ____________________
Assets ____________________
Number of Employees ____________
Organizational Affiliations:
Business Roundtable ____________
Defense Industry Initiative ____________

Individual Demographics

Job Title: ____________________
Number of years total work experience: ____________
Gender: Male Female
Age: ______

Section IV — Final Comments

If you would be willing to further discuss the impact of the Federal Sentencing Guidelines on Internal Audit, please attach your business card. (To maintain questionnaire response confidentiality, business cards will be kept separately, or if you prefer, you may send your card in a different envelope.) If you have any questions regarding this questionnaire, please contact Paul E. Fiorelli at (513) 745-2050 or Cynthia J. Rooney at (513) 745-2011. We appreciate your assistance and welcome any additional comments you may have.

APPENDIX B
ADDITIONAL ANALYSIS OF THE SURVEY

To obtain information from a broad group of individuals, a survey was conducted. The key results of the survey have been incorporated into this report. This appendix includes a more detailed description of the survey method and additional statistical analysis of the responses from internal auditors.

Survey Method

Questionnaires were mailed to a group of individuals selected from the membership records of The Institute of Internal Auditors (IIA). The target group included those who identified themselves in The IIA's database as the highest level internal auditor for their organization (typically, vice presidents). This group would likely be the most knowledgeable about the Federal Sentencing Guidelines (Guidelines) and the potential impact on internal auditing. Recipients could either complete the questionnaire themselves or deliver it to an appropriate individual. Questionnaires were mailed to the entire group (469 individuals in The IIA's database at that time). Of that group, 129 responses were returned resulting in a response rate of 27.5%.[1]

Respondents were also asked to pass an additional questionnaire along to the compliance officer, or other appropriate individual, within their organization. (Questionnaires were numbered such that the internal auditor and the compliance officer from the same organization would have corresponding questionnaire numbers.) From the distribution to compliance officers, 62 additional questionnaires were returned. To estimate the number of questionnaires distributed to compliance officers, the questionnaire asked internal auditors to indicate whether they had actually passed on the questionnaire. Of the 129 internal auditor respondents, 78 indicated that the extra questionnaire was passed on to the appropriate person. From that group of 78, there were 39 corresponding compliance officer questionnaires resulting in an approximate response rate of 50% from the compliance group.

Interestingly, corresponding compliance officer questionnaires were returned from three internal auditors who indicated that they did not forward the questionnaire and from seven who did not respond to the item regarding passing on the survey. Thirteen compliance officer questionnaires were received even though the corresponding internal auditor from that organization did not respond. This brought the total number of questionnaires received from compliance officers to 62. With the added 13 compliance officer questionnaires, with no corresponding internal audit response, a total of 142 organizations were represented.

Descriptive Statistics

The responses of the internal auditors were initially analyzed using basic descriptive statistics such as means and frequency distributions. In the next section, additional analysis compares responses based on various categories.

The first question on the survey asked respondents to indicate their familiarity with the Federal Sentencing Guidelines. Using a Likert 5-point scale with descriptive anchors on the extremes, respondents indicated that they were generally familiar with the Guidelines. With "extremely familiar" as the descriptive anchor for "5" and "not familiar" as "1", the mean response was 3.34. As shown in Table B-1, 10% of the respondents indicated that they were not familiar with the Guidelines, while over 55% rated their familiarity as a "4" or a "5".

[1]Since not all respondents completed every survey item, the actual number (n) of respondents for individual items is generally displayed on the tables.

Table B-1
Reported Familiarity with the Guidelines

		Rating Frequency (Percentage)				
	Mean	1 (Not Familiar)	2	3	4	5 (Extremely Familiar)
Familiarity (n = 128)	3.344	13 (10.2%)	17 (13.3%)	27 (21.1%)	55 (43%)	16 (12.5%)

When asked about the potential impact of the Guidelines on their organization, respondents were not convinced that there would be a significant impact. This seemed to confirm prior interview comments obtained by the researchers. As shown in Table B-2, only 3% indicated a significant impact, and 10% expected no impact.

Table B-2
Perceived Impact of the Guidelines

	Mean	1 (No Impact)	2	3	4	5 (Significant Impact)
Perceived Impact (n = 127)	2.709	13 (10.2%)	45 (35.4%)	39 (30.7%)	26 (20.5%)	4 (3.1%)

An additional question asked respondents to indicate key characteristics that influenced their perception of the potential impact of the Guidelines on their company. Table B-3 displays the reasons identified by the respondents, distributed by the ratings of the perceived impact. Respondents were allowed to select more than one item, thus the totals exceed the number of respondents. Of the 129 respondents, 38% (49 of 129) cited as a possible reason for the perceived impact "an analysis by the legal department." Almost 35% (45 of 129) indicated that federal, state, or industry regulations already satisfy the requirements. Reasons related to current regulations, sophistication of current systems, and few potential industry violations resulted in the lower mean scores (less than 2.7) regarding the perceived impact of the Guidelines on the organization.

Table B-3
Possible Reasons for Reported Impact, Distributed by Perceived Impact Rating

Reasons	Mean	Perceived Impact					Total
		1 (No Impact)	2	3	4	5 (Significant (Impact)	
Analysis by legal department	3.08	1	14	17	14	3	49
Federal, state, or industry regulations already satisfy the requirements	2.64	3	15	23	3	1	45
Size of the organization	3.23	1	8	12	17	2	40
Sophistication of current systems	2.68	0	18	17	5	0	40
Industry has few potential violations	2.44	2	8	6	2	0	18

Various roles were expected for the internal audit department related to the organization's compliance program based on prior interviews. As shown in Table B-4, about 30% of the respondents indicated that key members of Internal Audit were members of a compliance committee within their organization. Eleven organizations (8.7%) reported no compliance program, while 17 organizations (13%) indicated that internal audit was the compliance program. A large number of respondents (23%) described "other" involvement, such as "total corporate involvement in compliance including internal audit" and "compliance is separate from audit, but audit is significantly involved." Eight respondents included comments which indicated that in their organizations, internal audit monitors (audits/evaluates) the compliance program.

Table B-4
Reported Involvement of Internal Audit in the "Compliance Program"

	Frequency	Percentage
No compliance program in place, therefore no involvement of Internal Audit.	11	8.7%
No involvement, compliance program is separate from Internal Audit.	19	15.1%
Key members of Internal Audit are members of a compliance committee.	38	30.2%
Internal Audit is the compliance program.	17	13.5%
Other	29	23.0%
Multiple responses	12	9.5%
Total	126	100%

Respondents were asked to estimate the percentage of Internal Audit time spent on operational audits, financial audits, compliance audits, and other activities. Table B-5 presents measures of central tendency (mean, median, and mode) with minimum and maximum scores. The amount of time allocated to compliance audits was generally 20%, with a range of 1% to 90%. Two respondents categorized 100% of their activities as "other." Comments revealed that for one organization, "All audits were integrative," and for the other, "Only quality audits."

Table B-5
Reported Allocation of Internal Audit Activities

	Mean	Median	Mode	Minimum	Maximum
Operational Audits (n = 116)	38.7%	40%	50%	5%	95%
Financial Audits (n = 117)	36.0%	30%	20%	4%	90%
Compliance Audits (n = 105)	20.9%	20%	10%	1%	90%
Other Activities (n = 56)	21.4%	15%	10%	5%	100%

Respondents rated each of the seven minimum requirements of an effective compliance program regarding their organization's current compliance with the item were based on a 5-point scale which was anchored at the extremes (5 = "Very high" and 1 = "Very low"). The mean scores and the frequency distributions for each of the seven minimum requirements (R1-R7) are shown in Table B-6. Requirement 6, which relates to consistent and adequate discipline, received the lowest mean rating (3.32), with only 11.8% of the respondents rating their current compliance as "very high." Requirement 3, which requires due care in the avoidance of delegation of authority to those with a propensity to engage in illegal acts, received the highest mean rating (3.86).

Table B-6
Mean Scores and Frequency Distributions of Ratings of the Seven Minimum Requirements

		Frequency Distribution					
	Mean	1 (Very low)	2	3	4	5 (Very high)	Total
R1	3.68	3 (2.3%)	10 (7.8%)	37 (28.9%)	53 (41.4%)	25 (19.5%)	128 (100%)
R2	3.75	7 (5.5%)	13 (10.2%)	30 (23.6%)	32 (25.2%)	45 (35.4%)	127 (100%)
R3	3.86	3 (2.4%)	10 (7.9%)	27 (21.4%)	47 (37.3%)	39 (31%)	126 (100%)
R4	3.44	9 (7%)	21 (16.4%)	30 (23.4%)	41 (32%)	27 (21.1%)	128 (100%)
R5	3.55	7 (5.5%)	14 (10.9%)	38 (29.7%)	40 (31.3%)	29 (22.7%)	128 (100%)
R6	3.32	5 (3.9%)	17 (13.4%)	53 (41.7%)	37 (29.1%)	15 (11.8%)	127 (100%)
R7	3.70	3 (2.4%)	10 (7.9%)	34 (27%)	54 (42.9%)	25 (19.8%)	126 (100%)

Table B-7
Comparison of Ratings Based on Business Roundtable Members vs. Nonmembers

	Business Roundtable Members (N = 92)		Nonmembers (N = 36)		Statistical Significance[2]
	Mean	Std. Dev.	Mean	Std. Dev.	
R1	3.94	.92	3.58	.95	**
R2	4.19	1.12	3.57	1.19	***
R3	4.14	.99	3.76	1.02	*
R4	3.78	1.22	3.30	1.16	**
R5	3.72	1.11	3.47	1.12	None
R6	3.53	.94	3.23	.99	None
R7	3.94	.92	3.60	.96	*

*** Indicates statistical significance at the .01 level.
** Indicates statistical significance at the .05 level.
* Indicates statistical significance at the .1 level.

Investigation of Factors Influencing the Rating Scores

This section presents an investigation of possible factors which influence the rating scores of the seven minimum requirements. The first factor to be considered is membership in the Business Roundtable. Table B-7 presents the means and standard deviations for ratings of the seven requirements for members of the Business Roundtable and for nonmembers. As expected, in all cases, the mean scores of the Business Roundtable members were higher than the mean scores for nonmembers. The differences were statistically significant for five of the seven requirements.

[2]Based on the SAS statistical software package, using T-tests for both equal and unequal variance assumptions.

Comparisons of mean rating scores were also made based on size of the organization. Respondents were broken into two groups based on the median amount (i.e., half of the responses would be "large," the other half would be "small"). Table B-8 displays the results based on the size of reported revenues. For all of the requirements, the "large" organizations reported a higher mean. For six of the

Table B-8
Comparison of Ratings Based on Size of Revenues

	Large (more than $2,700,000 reported in revenues)		Small (less than $2,700,000 reported in revenues)		Statistical Significance
	Mean	Std. Dev.	Mean	Std. Dev.	
R1	3.91	0.88	3.37	0.94	***
R2	4.11	1.09	3.44	1.25	***
R3	4.00	0.84	3.66	1.20	None
R4	3.72	1.25	3.05	1.14	***
R5	3.85	0.96	3.19	1.10	***
R6	3.51	1.02	3.00	0.99	**
R7	3.85	0.78	3.44	1.07	**

*** Indicates statistical significance at the .01 level.
** Indicates statistical significance at the .05 level.
* Indicates statistical significance at the .1 level.

seven requirements, the differences were statistically significant. The same analysis process was repeated for size based on assets and size based on number of employees. Interestingly, the results based on number of employees were very similar,[3] although the analysis based on asset size reported higher means for the defined "large" group, none of the differences were statistically significant.

[3]"Large" organizations reported higher means than "small" organizations and the statistical analysis revealed that these differences were statistically significant for requirements 1, 2, 4, 5, and 6 at the .01 level (***) and for requirement 7 at the .05 level (**), while the differences for requirement 3 were not statistically significant.

Table B-9
Means of the Ratings by Industry

Variable	IND1 (N=16)	IND2 (N=1)	IND3 (N=33)	IND4 (N=15)	IND5 (N=2)	IND6 (N=6)	IND7 (N=29)	IND8 (N=9)	No Ind (N=13)
R1	4.05	3.00	3.58	3.67	5.00	3.33	3.48	3.89	3.69
R2	4.00	3.00	3.67	3.67	4.50	3.40	3.69	3.56	4.00
R3*	4.10	2.00	3.69	3.47	5.00	3.83	4.10	3.62	4.00
R4	3.80	2.00	3.52	3.07	4.50	3.33	3.21	3.56	3.54
R5	3.90	3.00	3.45	3.27	4.50	3.50	3.62	2.89	3.77
R6	3.60	2.00	3.30	2.86	4.00	3.00	3.38	3.11	3.54
R7	3.80	4.00	3.67	3.29	4.50	3.17	3.79	3.67	4.00

Industry Coding:

IND1 = Agriculture, Forestry, Fishing, Mining
IND2 = Construction
IND3 = Manufacturing
IND4 = Transportation, Communications, Public Utilities
IND5 = Wholesale Trade
IND6 = Retail Trade
IND7 = Finance, Insurance
IND8 = Services

* Indicates a statistical significance (at the .1 level) in the means of the industries using ANOVA.

Table B-9 presents the mean rating scores by industry. With very small numbers representing several industries, generalizations about industries are difficult. Using the analysis of variance (ANOVA) statistical technique, only R3 reported statistical significant differences in the means for the various groups.

The Finance and Insurance industry group (IND7) was separated into two groups, finance and insurance, to further consider possible differences. Table B-10 displays means for the two groups.

Table B-10
Means of the Ratings for the Finance and Insurance Industries

Variable	Finance (N = 21)	Insurance (N = 8)
R1	3.62	3.12
R2	3.86	3.25
R3	4.05	4.25
R4	3.33	2.87
R5	3.81	3.13
R6	3.52	3.00
R7	3.95	3.29

The respondents indicated an overall mean familiarity score of 3.34 on a 5-point scale. To explore the possible impact of familiarity with the standards on the rating of the variables, mean rating scores for the various levels of indicated familiarity were determined. Table B-11 displays the results. Analysis of variance (ANOVA) was used to consider the statistical significance of the rating

Table B-11
Means of the Ratings by Familiarity

Variable	1 (N = 12)	2 (N = 17)	3 (N = 27)	4 (N = 55)	5 (N = 16)
R1	4.05	3.00	3.58	3.67	5.00
R2	4.00	3.00	3.67	3.67	4.50
R3	4.10	2.00	3.69	3.47	5.00
R4	3.80	2.00	3.52	3.07	4.50
R5	3.90	3.00	3.45	3.27	4.50
R6	3.60	2.00	3.30	2.86	4.00
R7	3.80	4.00	3.67	3.29	4.50

scores given the level of familiarity. Table B-12 indicates that for six of the seven minimum guidelines, the differences in scores based on level of familiarity were statistically significant.

Rating scores were also categorized by the role of internal audit in the compliance program. Initial analysis of this variable was presented in Table B-4. Mean scores of the ratings were obtained for

Table B-12
ANOVA Results on Impact Rating Scores
Based on Familiarity with the Guidelines

		Sum of Squares (SS)	Degrees of Freedom (DF)	Mean Square (MS)	F
R1	Between Ss	10.68	4	2.67	3.11**
	Within Ss	104.72	122	.86	
R2	Between Ss	20.23	4	5.06	3.97***
	Within Ss	154.10	121	1.27	
R3	Between Ss	10.52	4	2.63	2.65**
	Within Ss	118.89	120	.99	
R4	Between Ss	14.81	4	3.70	2.81**
	Within Ss	160.70	122	1.32	
R5	Between Ss	7.10	4	1.77	1.48
	Within Ss	146.08	122	1.20	
R6	Between Ss	8.31	4	2.08	2.33*
	Within Ss	107.69	121	.89	
R7	Between Ss	13.79	4	3.45	4.43***
	Within Ss	93.41	120	.78	

*** Indicates statistical significance at the .01 level.
** Indicates statistical significance at the .05 level.
* Indicates statistical significance at the .1 level.

Table B-13
Rating Scores Categorized by Involvement of Internal Audit in the Compliance Program

	No compliance program, no internal audit involvement. (n = 10)	Compliance program separate from internal audit, no internal audit involvement. (n = 19)	Key members of internal audit are members of a compliance committee. (n = 38)	Internal audit is the compliance committee. (n = 17)
R1	2.50	3.74	3.89	3.76
R2	2.10	3.79	4.13	3.50
R3	2.80	3.68	4.08	4.00
R4	1.90	3.47	3.71	3.35
R5	2.10	3.74	3.76	3.59
R6	2.20	3.32	3.49	3.41
R7	2.30	3.68	4.03	3.82

the various categories. As displayed in Table B-13, scores for the group with "no compliance program" were lower than the other three groups. The higher scores were reported for the group where key members of internal audit were members of a compliance committee. This is probably because these organizations have already committed substantial efforts to establishing an effective compliance program.

An alternate measure of Internal Audit's involvement with the seven minimum requirements was obtained by asking respondents to indicate on a 5 point scale the level of their involvement in three types of activities (design, monitoring, and investigation of reported failures) for each of the requirements as appropriate. The results, displayed in Table B-14, indicate that internal audit is more likely to be involved in monitoring and investigating reported failures as opposed to design activities. This relationship was observed for activities related to each applicable requirement.

Table B-14
Internal Audit's Involvement with Design, Monitoring, and Investigation of Reported Failures Related to Each of the Seven Minimum Requirements

	Mean Scores for Involvement (Based on 5-point scale: 5 = very involved; 1 = not involved)		
Activities Related to:	Design	Monitoring	Investigation of reported failures
Requirement 1	3.14	3.82	3.92
Requirement 2	n/a	n/a	n/a
Requirement 3	3.05	3.58	3.83
Requirement 4	n/a	n/a	n/a
Requirement 5	3.34	3.74	3.98
Requirement 6	n/a	n/a	n/a
Requirement 7	3.55	3.85	n/a

APPENDIX C
FREEDOMS AND OBLIGATIONS:
SEARS SHARED BELIEFS, LEADERSHIP PRINCIPLES, AND CODE OF BUSINESS CONDUCT

A Letter from the Chairman

Dear Sears Manager:

Freedoms and Obligations are important concepts. Every day you face dozens of decisions and issues that require you to instinctively use your freedoms and meet your obligations.

And yet, historically, Sears has asked you to depend too heavily on a thick set of complex rules.

That has now changed!

Today, we face a rapidly changing retail environment where we must focus totally on the customer. Sears future depends on us creating a culture where all associates have the knowledge and support they need to act independently and appropriately.

Our Shared Beliefs, Leadership Principles, and *Code of Business Conduct* provide you with a sound base for your decision making responsibilities.

I request that you then take personal responsibility for your unit, your customers, and your decisions and, as appropriate, transfer responsibility to your colleagues.

This is another building block in our company's transformation, signifying our belief that all of our people add value to our business every day.

Sincerely,

Arthur C. Martinez
Chairman and CEO

Shared Beliefs Support Sears Vision as a Compelling Place to Shop, Work and Invest

Passion for the Customer

We believe that it's everyone's responsibility to serve and satisfy every Sears customer. We build lasting relationships with these customers by creating experiences that make Sears their first choice. We keep our promises and proudly support "Satisfaction guaranteed, or your money back."

We have developed a trust with our customers based on integrity and we are committed to strengthening that trust. Through partnership and teamwork, we provide quality merchandise and services that meet our customers' expectations and enrich their quality of life. We vow to listen to our customers and respond.

We strive for speed and simplicity in the way we do our jobs. This will facilitate and enhance the customer's shopping experience.

Our People Add Value

Our people and their ideas and decisions are what ultimately create value for our customers.

We value each person's unique character and contribution. We respect the dignity and potential of all our people and we strongly encourage their growth. We treat each person fairly and honestly. We communicate openly.

We face the competition as a team and we share in the rewards of our success.

Performance Leadership

We recognize our obligation to our stockholders: profitable growth and superior total shareholder return. We believe that industry leading performance can only be achieved if we act as owners who are accountable for their actions.

We value innovation. We accept the risks and mistakes that can result from trying new ideas as an investment in future performance and growth.

Leadership Principles

Straightforward Guidelines for Managers

How to Best Use this Information

No one has all the answers. Sears expects you to balance the resources you have to make decisions.

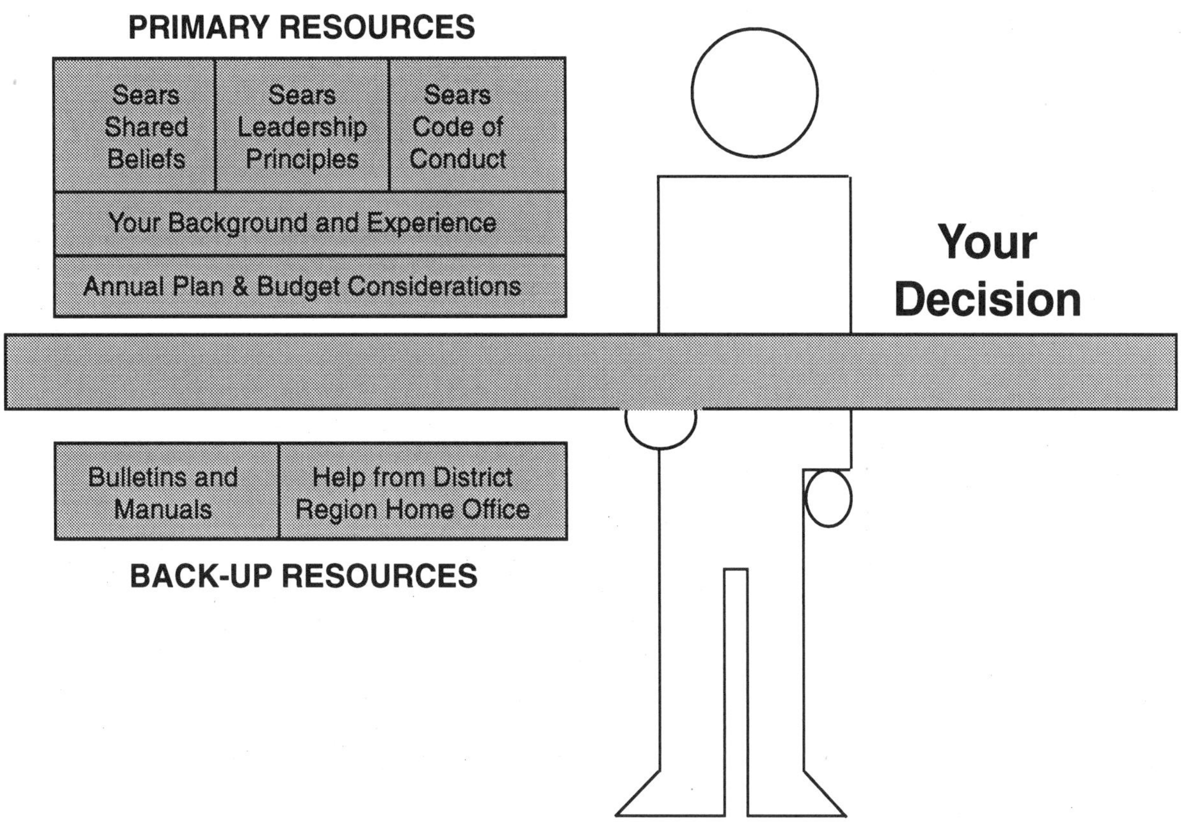

Empowering Managers

Carefully read all the material in this brochure, as well as the "Code of Business Conduct" booklet. If you don't understand something, ask. Sears has a support network of experts to help you. Share this information with people at your facility who come to you with questions, or, who themselves should be aware of the material.

Opportunity

Like most large companies, Sears developed a thick set of procedures over the years. Originally intended to help managers solve problems, they grew complex and burdensome, and actually stifled progress in some situations. Managers' hands were frequently tied.

But times have changed and so has Sears. In today's economy, we must be more competitive than ever. We need the full brain power of each manager and associate to build a truly better Sears.

Sears believes that the responsibility and authority to satisfy customers is best given to those who deal with customers on a daily basis. This is an exciting, opportune time to be a Sears manager and part of the Sears team. You are being asked to be more innovative — to take greater responsibility for local decision making.

Sears, however, doesn't intend to simply provide you authority and responsibility for making decisions. It wouldn't be fair to merely assign you this obligation or to expect that your experience and best judgment are always sufficient. You must develop skills that will improve your decision making capabilities. Sears shares this responsibility with you.

Sears has put together this booklet which contains straightforward advice. We want to help you think through the tough situations — to determine the best solution. These guidelines won't solve every problem, but they'll set you in the right direction. To help you locate information quickly — when you need it — the guidelines have been arranged according to major Sears functions.

To begin with, there are some general principles to get you started:

- If you can't please everybody — please the customer first.
- Apply your best judgment based on the guideline in this booklet and the Code of Business Conduct. When in doubt, consult the support network of experts available to you.
- If you learn something from a mistake, it wasn't all bad — especially if you teach others.
- Remove any barriers that stand between your unit and another Sears organization. Work with your associates to build a better Sears.

The Flip Side of Empowerment

Each of us is judged by the quality of our choices. We are accountable for our decisions and we must be fully aware of all the people we're responsible to.

Responsibility

Sears, however, isn't simply dropping all the rules and giving everyone free rein. Empowerment includes acting in Sears best interests. It is extended to those who have demonstrated their maturity and judgment.

Like any other opportunity, empowerment comes with a string attached: *you are expected to make correct decisions.*

We answer to six constituencies; that is, people who have a stake in the quality of our decisions:

- millions of customers a year who rely on Sears for value,
- our associates who create this value,
- Sears shareholders around the world,
- countless suppliers of merchandise, services and materials,
- the communities who are good neighbors to our stores, and
- local, county, state and federal governments and agencies.

Practically every decision you make or conclusion you reach will directly concern several of these groups. Some issues, safety, for example, affect all six. As a result, these constituencies must be a factor in your decision making.

Carefully read the materials in this package. They're designed as guidelines to help you when you're facing a tough situation.

Accounting and Finance

Accounting & Finance supports Sears managers by designing, measuring and reporting key performance information.

- Every Sears associate is responsible for the integrity of information.
- Insure that all data are accurate and timely. Reporting your performance information is a serious responsibility.
- Be sure reports accurately reflect what is happening in your business.
- Question the necessity of your reports. If you don't need the report — speak up!

Asset Protection and Safety

- Take immediate action in a hazardous situation. Use your best judgment. You are responsible for the lives and well being of your associates and customers. Think of them first.
- Provide associates a safe work area, safe job procedures and safety hazard training.
- Provide customers a safe place to shop.
- Safeguard Sears customers, associates, merchandise, supplies and property. Sears assets also include company and customer information, as well as our reputation.
- Create an atmosphere where safety procedures are respected and followed by all associates.
- Identify — and either reduce or eliminate — safety and health hazards at work. This applies to all Sears associates.
- Carefully train associates who encounter hazardous substances or conditions in their work area.
- Record and report all accidents.

The Asset Protection department is responsible for helping managers create a safe working and shopping environment and for helping managers protect Sears merchandise, property and other resources.

Buying and Merchandising Practices

Sears merchandising teams are responsible for providing the right product, of the right quality, at the right time, in the right quantities, at a right cost to Sears, so that Sears can provide value to our customers.

- Deliver to customers what Sears promises.
- Live the Value Equation: Sears customers deserve high quality merchandise and services at a fair price.
- Develop long-term relationships with your customers to insure everyone's success.
- Find ways to cut costs without sacrificing quality. This is the mark of a great manager.
- Provide information to help buyers and vendors improve their merchandise and services. Your feedback is critical.
- Inspire your associates — be a source of special support. All associates require training, but those who deal directly with customers require special assistance to make Sears a compelling place to shop. Your insights and experience can be invaluable.
- Solicit feedback from associates and customers to improve your own customer service skills.

Credit

Sears Credit provides more services to Sears customers than many people realize. The Sears Card offers convenience, security, savings, value and recognition that increase customer satisfaction and improve shareholder value.

- Treat all account applicants in a fair and impartial manner.
- Regard all Sears account and applicant information as strictly confidential.

The Environment

Sears position is very clear: implement programs and procedures to meet or exceed environmental laws and regulations. Know the laws and follow them.

In a hazardous situation, take immediate action. As with safety issues, you are responsible for the lives and well being of your associates and customers. Facilities Planning can help you make the right decision to prevent problems.

- Contact the Law department or your district manager if you're in doubt on a compliance issue.
- Encourage the development of products and packaging designed to be reused or recycled — or that minimize waste. This applies to service vendors, too. It's another way Sears helps to protect the environment.
- Dispose of waste safely and responsibly. Our communities and people expect us to.
- Think "energy efficiency" — it's fundamental to Sears.

Ethics and Business Policy

Sears holds a position of trust with our customers, associates, shareholders, communities, suppliers and government agencies. The Office of Ethics and Business Policy is responsible for providing clear, simple guidelines as tools to help you make effective decisions.

- Help prevent illegal or unethical behavior. Keep an eye out for questionable behavior.
- Assure your associates that they can report unethical behavior without fear of retaliation.
- Call 1-800-8-ASSIST for easy to use, free advice to resolve ethical or policy questions and to clarify questionable situations.
- Explain Sears ethical philosophy to associates. Help them understand this material. They'll do a better job.
- Help associates do the right things for the right reasons. Encourage them to take the high road through your example.

Human Resources

Managers are accountable for creating an environment where "Sears people add value!" Human Resources supports that effort.

- Recruit, train, retain and promote the most qualified people with the skills and attitude necessary for the job — people who will contribute to Sears. Bright, outgoing, positive people, for example, have the natural skills for dealing with customers. Retail experience is helpful, but job procedures can be learned — look for the best people first.
- Treat all associates with respect and dignity.
- Provide leadership that is fair and consistent.
- Protect the confidentiality and privacy of all associates.
- Listen carefully to your associates and value their contributions. Great leaders learn from their people.
- Reward people who add value to Sears. Sears calls for pay and benefits levels to be fair to our associates and competitive with other retailers.
- Support Sears economic literacy goal. Associates must understand the importance of customer satisfaction and cost reduction.
- Se the example for job performance and personal behavior. You cannot expect more than you give.
- Provide honest performance feedback and take appropriate action when improvement is required. Proper performance appraisals are necessary for associate development.
- Recognize excellence among your associates. Encourage these people to fully develop their skills.
- Empower associates to try new ideas. Encourage your associates according to their personal capabilities.
- Insure that your associates are properly trained to provide the professional service our customers expect.
- Recognize the diversity of your Sears community. Reflect it in the way your store does business. The cultural heritage of your store's associates should represent this diversity, as well.

Information Services

Information Services provides technology and data processing that allow Sears to meet strategic business objectives.

- Know how to take full advantage of the information resources available to you. This will improve the quality of your decisions and make your job much easier.
- Prevent the use of unauthorized software. Sears uses legally licensed software only. Units receive this software and support from Information Services. Call them with any questions.
- Safeguard important business information. Associates should understand that certain information is confidential and not available to everyone.
- Preserve data integrity by providing controls and support that result in accurate data input and protection. Information is a decision making resource, but only if it's accurate.

Internal Audit and Control

Internal Audit is Sears way of fulfilling its requirement to develop, implement and monitor internal control systems to insure: effective and efficient operations; reliable financial reporting; the safety of our assets and resources; and compliance with the law and other regulations.

- Understand that internal controls are essential to any organization. Internal controls provide extremely useful information — the key to empowerment. If you're to be effective, Sears systems of internal controls and procedures must be fully in effect at your unit.
- If you suspect that an internal control program is ineffective, for any reason, contact Internal Audit. If you're right, they'll help you correct it. If not, you've learned more about your job.

Investor Relations

Investor Relations provides accurate, dependable and consistent information to enable securities analysts, investors and potential investors to better understand our current and long range business. This communications process permits Sears securities to achieve a market value consistent with our operating performance and outlook. Because of federal laws regarding investor related activities, Sears managers and associates must follow very strict rules and regulations.

- All financial analyst, investor or potential investor contact is to be made through Investor Relations.
- Your answer to rumors regarding Sears business or prospects is "As a matter of policy, we do not comment on rumors or speculation." Refer questions and callers to Investor Relations.
- Federal law prohibits the purchase or sale of stocks or other securities by anyone who has material, nonpublic (or "insider") information regarding those securities.
- Federal law also prohibits sharing or "tipping" inside information to someone who might use that information to trade in those securities.
- Be aware that if you have inside information on Sears or any company we do business with, you cannot trade in those securities or "tip" that information to anyone until the information is publicly disclosed. The penalties can be severe, including fines and imprisonment.

Law and Government Affairs

Although you are empowered to make numerous decisions, Sears policies support the law. When it comes to legal and governmental practices, on most points, you have few or no options:

- When in doubt about legal issues, check with the Law department. They not only clarify issues, but they can solve problems, too.
- Instruct your associates on the importance of Sears legal and business policy issues. Help them understand how and when to seek advice.
- Cooperate fully with the Law department and outside counsel hired by Sears. Be truthful and accurate.
- Send notices of lawsuits and other legal proceedings by overnight mail to the Law department.
- Sears Law department has sole authority to hire outside legal counsel.
- Sears cooperates with all reasonable requests from government agencies at all levels. However, the requests are handled by the Law department. If government officials request information from you — contact the Law department immediately.
- You might be approached for support in a local, state, or federal election or a referendum or lobbying effort. Associates and managers cannot contribute Sears money, property, labor or services to any candidate or political party without approval from Governmental Affairs.

Laws, regulations and ordinances govern practically every aspect of Sears business practices. Sears Law department helps managers prevent legal problems. The Law department manages litigation and claims, negotiates documents, and reviews and approves contracts before they are signed. Governmental Affairs tracks legislation affecting the company and presents Sears point of view to protect the interests of our customers, associates and shareholders.

Logistics

Sears Logistics Group plans and carries out systems to deliver merchandise to our customers in the fastest and most economical way.

- On most big ticket sales, home delivery is our last link with the customer. Promise only what you can deliver and when you can deliver it. Make it a great lasting impression!

- Optimize logistical costs by balancing transportation, distribution and store operating expenses. Consider this balance when making decisions on inventory, shuttle frequency, or return handling.

- Requests for special delivery service can be extremely costly. Carefully weigh all factors before making your decision.

- Open and clear two-way communication between your servicing distribution center and you are fundamental to smooth logistics operations.

Marketing and Advertising

Marketing and Advertising work to build the positive, motivating image of Sears as a compelling place for our target customer to shop. This helps create store traffic and strengthens long-term bonds with the people who pay our salaries. Sears Customer Information and Research gathers reliable data to help us develop a better understanding of our customers.

- Our advertising is an honest, legitimate and tasteful invitation to the customer to shop at our stores. Effective Sears advertising and promotions are straightforward and clearly understood.

- Insure that in-store signs are properly placed, displayed at the right time, and that price and product information are accurate.

- Your customers expect display prices to be consistent with prices in our sales terminals.

- Listen carefully to your customers and honor their wishes. Sears values their opinions. This is yet another means of developing long-term relationships.

Product Services

Product Services is the nation's largest provider of in-home appliance installation and maintenance services.

- If it's not broken, don't fix it.
- If you can prolong the life of the merchandise and avoid future inconvenience for the customer, do so.
- If it's not worth fixing, give the customer your best advice.
- If it's not timely, it's not service.
- Communicate honestly and directly to our customers. It's easier to explain disappointing news in the beginning than to explain why their expectations were not met.

Public Affairs

Public Affairs is Sears voice to associates, customers, shareholders, media representatives and the public at large.

- It's better that associates hear news about Sears from you, rather than the news media.
- Speak honestly and promptly with your associates.
- Help build Sears reputation in your area. You are the local role model for community relations — it's your store and it's your community. Associates look to you for direction. Sears true spirit shines most brightly through community and volunteer programs.
- On local issues, you're the best spokesperson for Sears. As long as the information is not competitive or confidential, speak honestly and openly with the media.
- Media Relations coordinates media contact on all sensitive, national, financial or legal matters.

Real Estate and Facilities Planning

Real Estate is responsible for the strategic placement of all Sears stores and other facilities for long-term business success. Facilities Planning builds and remodels stores, plans visual presentation of merchandise and purchases all equipment and fixtures for our stores.

- Real Estate and Facilities Planning are your partners in preserving and improving the value of the Sears property you manage.
- Real estate directors negotiate the purchase and lease of new store locations. Property managers negotiate real estate matters for existing locations.
- Contact Facilities Planning to resolve questions about space planning and allocation, ordering equipment, major maintenance or construction and environmental matters.
- As an active leader in your business community, you know a great deal about local real estate. Information about local property issues of potential interest to Sears should be passed along to the Real Estate department.

Retail Store Operations

Retail Store Operations provides systems and procedures assistance, as well as support in expense control and maintaining the physical environment.

- You're the source for sales, profits and customer satisfaction leadership. Store Operations provides you many of the tools you need.
- You be the judge. Is Retail Store Operations providing you the support to improve customer satisfaction, associate productivity and financial returns? If not, they'll know sooner if you call them.
- Balancing the need to improve customer service with the need to reduce costs requires your most delicate touch. If you have to sacrifice one of the two, remember that happy customers write letters; they tell their friends; and they come back time and time again.

Risk Management

Risk Management helps managers control the cost of losses from Sears operations and assets through self-insurance, transfer of risk to suppliers of goods and services, and by purchasing insurance.

- When considering any activities outside of normal merchandising, such as special events or parking lot sales, contact Risk Management.
- Request certificates of insurance and surety bonds from Risk Management.

Sales Practices

Sears has a wonderful reputation with the public. Since we first started business in 1886, the cornerstone of our company has been a commitment to treat our customers fairly and consistently.

- Clearly explain Sears policy of "Satisfaction Guaranteed or Your Money Back" to all associates:

  If, for any reason, you are not satisfied with your purchase from Sears, return it with your receipt within a reasonable period of time from the date of purchase for a full refund or exchange.

  If you are not satisfied with your purchase, even after a reasonable period of time from the date of purchase, please let us know. We want to make an adjustment you will consider fair.

  Within these two guidelines, your associates are authorized to satisfy the customer through full or partial refund or an exchange.

- If your associate cannot satisfy the customer, you should.
- Remember: anything spoken or written about Sears products or services, whether it's advertising, sales presentations, signs, packaging or press releases, will always be clear, truthful, accurate, supportable and consistent with accepted standards of good taste.

Final Thoughts

Sears has anticipated a few questions you might have at this point:

Does the company really want me to have all this freedom?
Yes — Sears really means it. We're in a new, extremely competitive era. Our associates closest to the customer must be free to make winning decisions. Without responsible local decision-making, we'll never complete the transformation necessary to win in this new, aggressive atmosphere.

What if I need help?
Everyone needs help from time to time. The very best managers are those who know when to seek guidance or support.

To make good decisions, you need information. Aren't you saying, "I have to know it all?"
Certainly not. But you do need to know where to find the information to help you make the decision. Consider help from several sources, including:

- Other managers. Sometimes just discussing an issue makes it easier to resolve.
- District and region support teams. They know your markets and problems.
- Your Store Support team at Hoffman Estates. We serve Sears customers by serving *you.*
- If you need further guidance, refer to the directions on E-mail to identify appropriate experts.

Sears transformation is in your hands. Make it happen!

Leadership Model

Code of Business Conduct

The Business Reputation of Sears Rests with Each Associate

Letter from the Chairman

An enduring set of values is fundamental to the way in which we conduct our business at Sears, Roebuck and Co. Sears associates are expected to deal honestly, responsibly and fairly with everyone with whom we do business.

These are not new ideas at Sears, but it is vital that each and every associate make a personal commitment to uphold them. We must each work hard to achieve the highest standards of ethical business conduct — "the high road" — and to further the bond of trust we enjoy with our customers, suppliers, investors, government officials and fellow associates.

The basic guideline we are asked to observe as we carry out our duties for Sears is a simple one: If ever in doubt about the proper course of action, take the high road.

Arthur C. Martinez
Chairman and CEO

A Century-Old Bond of Trust

Guidelines for Making Ethical Decisions:

1. Is it Legal?
2. Is it Within Sears Beliefs and Policies?
3. Is it Right/Fair/Appropriate?
4. Would I Want Everyone to Know About This?
5. How Will I Feel About Myself?

"The whole business reputation of Sears, Roebuck and Co. rests in the hands of our people." That is what our 1896 employee handbook said, and it is no less true today. The reputation of our company and its associates for fair and honest dealing — with customers, vendors, suppliers, shareholders and with one another — is our greatest asset.

Trust, coupled with value and outstanding customer service, was an unbeatable combination a century ago when Richard Sears started our company. It still is. We have earned the bond of trust we enjoy with our customers by dealing honestly and fairly through the years with everyone with whom we do business. And as Sears associates, we continue to earn that trust every day, in every transaction, at every Sears location.

We all have a stake in the reputation of Sears, Roebuck and Co. as a compelling place to shop, work and invest. Maintaining our good name is our shared responsibility. It is up to each of us to enhance and protect this reputation.

Introduction

Purpose of this Booklet

This Code of Conduct describes the commitment of Sears, Roebuck and Co. to a set of high ethical standards. As Sears associates, we must become familiar with these guidelines and should apply them, in letter and in spirit.

Where to Seek Guidance

If this booklet does not answer your questions adequately, contact your manager for guidance. If you feel it is inappropriate to discuss a problem with your manager, contact your Human Resource manager or Sears Office of Ethics and Business Policy. Guidance is available through the Ethics Assist Line by calling 1-800-8ASSIST.

Reporting Non-Compliance

If you have knowledge of a violation of Sears policy or any legal requirement, you have an obligation to report it to your manager or the Sears Office of Ethics and Business Policy at 1-800-8ASSIST. You may report violations knowing that Sears will not allow retaliation against you for such reporting.

Following This Code

All Sears associates must abide by this Code of Conduct. No one is an exception. This is a condition of employment.

1•800•8ASSIST

1-800-827-7478

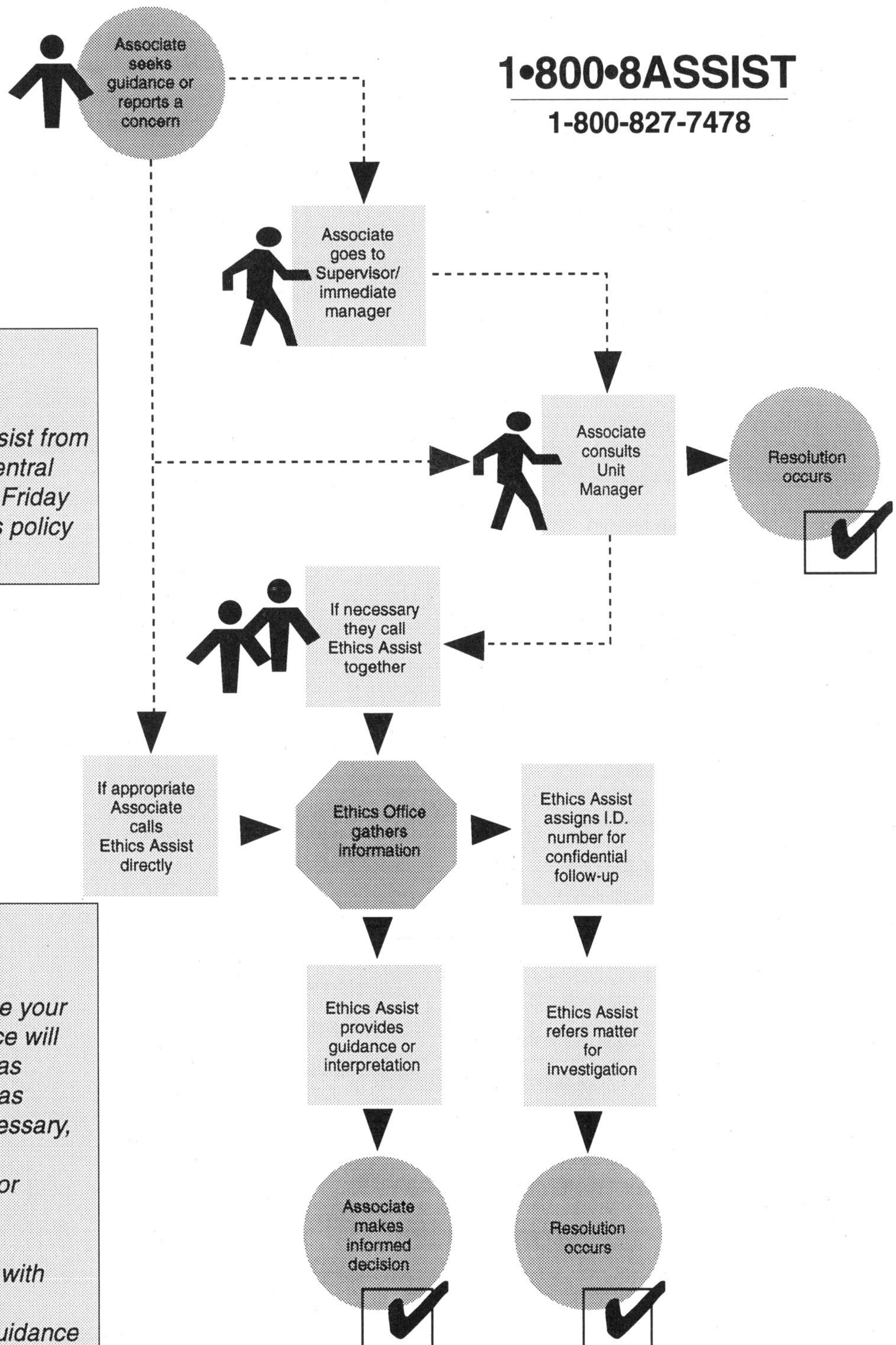

Guidance and Straight Answers

You can call Ethics Assist from 9:00 am to 4:00 pm Central Time Monday through Friday with ethics or business policy issues.

Confidential Assistance

You do not have to give your name. The Ethics Office will handle your inquiry in as confidential a manner as practicable, and if necessary, will assign you an identification number for confidential follow-up.

Ethics Assist can help with these types of calls:

- *Interpretation or guidance about company policy*
- *Code of Conduct issues*
- *Workplace harassment/ discrimination*
- *Selling practices*
- *Theft*
- *General ethics questions*

Fair Dealing

We always strive to treat our customers and all others with whom we do business fairly and honestly. We have remained in business for so long because our customers know that they can count on our honesty and fairness. Whether doing business with customers or suppliers, all Sears associates are expected to deal fairly and honestly and to maintain the highest ethical standards.

Our Selling Practices

Sears long-term success depends on satisfied customers and the foundation of Sears customer relationships has been our pledge of "Satisfaction Guaranteed or Your Money Back." Unethical sales practices create ill will and result in the loss of customer trust. Since a reputation for fair dealing must be earned every day, with every sale, it is critical that we always deal with our customers honestly and truthfully and show a genuine concern for their needs.

We must always describe products and services accurately. Our customers benefit when we sell responsibly by explaining how our products and services meet their needs. As Sears associates, we have an obligation to be well-informed about the performance, pricing, features and quality of the products and services we sell. Whether describing Sears products or comparing Sears products to those offered by competition, we should always be accurate and never misrepresent or "stretch" the truth.

Sears advertisements are sincere, good faith offers to sell the advertised merchandise. We must always represent advertised items in a favorable light and make an affirmative offer to sell them. Failing to make a good faith offer to sell, or intentionally discouraging customers from purchasing advertised items in order to "switch" them to other merchandise may constitute "bait and switch" sales tactics which are contrary to both Sears policy and the law.

Q: *While ringing up a sale recently, I noticed that an item was mismarked and the customer was being overcharged. The customer did not seem to notice, and there were many people waiting in line. Would it be all right not to mention the error?*

A: No, it is never acceptable to overcharge a customer. Charge the customer the correct price and advise your manager that the item is mismarked.

Q: *I am a sales manager. In conducting a routine package check, I find that merchandise sold by one associate to a fellow associate has not been charged or charged incorrectly. What should I do?*

A: Both associates are responsible for the accuracy of this transaction. Contact Asset Protection personnel to interview both associates. Have the associate who made the purchase pay the amount due. Mistakes can happen, but such activity may indicate theft.

> **Q:** *I generally know the warranty for the products I sell. What is the policy if a customer asks to see the warranty? Do I always need to look up the exact warranty terms?*
>
> **A:** Yes. If the customer asks to see the warranty, you are obligated under federal law to show the customer its text before they purchase.

Our customers place great reliance on our product performance claims when deciding whether to purchase from Sears. Such claims must be accurate and supported by fact.

Sears must always make its own decisions about pricing. Federal and state antitrust laws prohibit competitors from agreeing with each other to set or stabilize prices at which they purchase or sell products. The law also forbids agreeing with our licensees regarding specific prices for products and services they sell under the Sears name. We are also prohibited from agreeing with suppliers on retail selling prices of products Sears purchases from them.

Our Buying Practices

The company's continuing success depends in part on strong suppliers capable of providing Sears with quality merchandise at competitive costs. Suppliers must be selected on the basis of the best interests of Sears. Never make vendor selections based upon your personal interests.

Sears associates who make buying decisions must be well-informed about the suppliers they select and must always consider their financial condition, trade reputation and reliability. We will deal only with suppliers who share Sears commitment to the highest ethical business standards and who have proven records of supplying safe, quality products or services that conform with the law. When purchasing goods not produced in the United States, the production facilities, business and labor practices, and merchandise of our suppliers must comply with all applicable local and United States law.

> **Q:** *I think a competitor is misstating the performance on a product it offers. I don't want to lose the sale. Can I "talk up" or stretch the performance of the Sears product to clinch the sale?*
>
> **A:** No. The capabilities of the Sears product must always be accurately described. If you know the performance of the competitor's item, you should correct any misinformation the customer may have in a factual manner, without accusing the competitor of lying.

Conduct in the Workplace

Sears is committed to providing a safe, orderly, diverse and tolerant work environment, free of discrimination and harassment. As Sears associates, we are expected to grant others the same respect, cooperation and dignity we wish for ourselves.

Job Expectations

We all need to come to work each day ready to perform our jobs ethically and in a way that serves our customers and adds value to our shareholders. We should protect Sears assets and its good name. Managers have a special responsibility to make fair decisions, encourage ethical behavior by associates, and serve as examples to all associates.

Equal Employment Opportunity and Affirmative Action

Discriminating against any Sears associate or any person with whom we have business dealings on the basis of race, color, religion, sex, age, marital status, national origin, sexual orientation, disability or veteran status is not permitted. This applies to all areas of employment including hiring, training, advancement, compensation, benefits, discipline and termination.

Q: *My manager has set quotas for the sale of Maintenance Agreements (MAs) and implied my job is at stake if I don't meet them. Is this company policy?*

A: No. While MA or Stain Protection Agreement (SPA) sales are one important measurement of performance, a manager may not make this the sole factor in evaluating your performance.

Q: *My supervisor has asked me several times to go with him and other associates to a bar for a drink after work. I have refused, but I feel I am being pressured to join these social events. What should I do?*

A: If you do not desire to attend such events, advise your supervisor of this and ask that the invitations stop. If this conduct persists, contact the Ethics Office at 1-800-8ASSIST or your supervisor's supervisor.

Sears has an Affirmative Action Program that not only meets federal, state, and local requirements but also strives to place Sears in an affirmative action leadership position. Sears associates are expected to help make our equal employment opportunity and affirmative action programs effective throughout the company.

Workplace Harassment

Harassment in the workplace is strictly prohibited and will not be tolerated. Unwelcome advances, such as requests for sexual favors and other verbal or physical conduct of a sexual nature, may be forms of sexual harassment. In addition, conduct that may create an uncomfortable situation, such as inappropriate comments, jokes, intimidation, or physical contact, may be forms of workplace harassment. Associates should avoid any actions or words that might be interpreted by another as harassment.

Alcohol and Substance Abuse

Sears is committed to a drug- and alcohol-free workplace. Any associate who uses, distributes or is under the influence of alcohol or illegal drugs in the workplace is in violation of Sears policy. All associates are also responsible for reporting any improper use or distribution of alcohol or illegal drugs in the workplace. Associates are encouraged to seek treatment for drug or alcohol related problems. Full-time and regular part-time associates can do so through the strictly confidential Employee Assistance Program, which can be reached by calling 1-800-424-4732.

Q: *One of the sales associates in the department I supervise always dresses in a very sloppy and unpleasant manner. Can I suggest a better style of dress, or will this be considered harassment?*

A: Appropriate dress is important for all associates. Advise the associate of our general dress code standards.

Q: *May I have a drink on my lunch break or before I report to work? They both are on my time.*

A: No. The consumption of alcohol at those times can influence your job performance.

Conflicts of Interests

When we are engaged in Sears business, we are expected to act in the company's best interests. We must avoid conflicts of interest in which we use our position at Sears to benefit personally or to benefit someone else at Sears expense. We must also avoid the appearance of such conflicts and should never act through someone else to violate this policy.

Outside Employment

No salaried associates may work for Sears competitors or for vendors or other companies doing business with Sears. Salaried associates should also seek approval if they plan to work independently or to perform significant voluntary or charitable work that may affect their responsibilities at Sears.

An hourly associate who wishes to work for a Sears competitor, vendor or other company doing business with Sears must seek the guidance and approval of their unit manager. Permission may be granted, provided the outside position:

- Does not interfere with an associate's ability to discharge his or her responsibilities;
- Does not conflict or appear to conflict with work at Sears;
- Does not pose a risk of transmitting confidential information to outsiders.

Personal Investments

We are all expected to make our personal investments in a way that avoids the use, for personal gain, of any non-public material information obtained in the course of our work at Sears. Although we may invest in companies that do business with Sears, we may not do so if we are personally involved in significant decisions relating to those companies. We should never make a personal investment in a company when we have the ability to influence its relationship with Sears. Where personal gain could conflict or appear to conflict with Sears duties, full written disclosure to our managers is required.

Q: *I am a Product Services technician with the responsibility to service a variety of major brand products. Can I perform similar independent service work during my off-hours?*

A: Yes you may, but in no case may you solicit personal work from Sears customers.

Q: *May I, as a Sears manager, invest directly in the stock of a significant retail competitor?*

A: While you may legally make such investments, a material investment in another retailer is not consistent with our competitive goals.

Q: *A stockbroker has suggested an investment in a new company. Although I am not directly involved, I am aware of confidential negotiations that might result in that company becoming a significant Sears source. May I follow the stockbroker's advice?*

A: No. Since you have some knowledge of these confidential negotiations, following the stockbroker's advice might be considered prohibited insider trading.

> **Q:** *May my spouse accompany me on a vendor sponsored business trip?*
>
> **A:** Yes, provided your family or Sears pays for your spouse's expenses. You may not accept hospitality for your spouse from an existing or prospective supplier.

Gifts and Benefits

We should never receive any improper benefit, monetary or otherwise, from an organization that is a supplier to Sears, that seeks to do business with Sears, or that is a Sears competitor. We may not influence or participate in the management of any such business except when directly authorized by Sears. We also may not influence any other businesses improperly by offering them gifts or benefits.

An improper benefit may include anything of value offered to us in an attempt to inappropriately influence our business judgment. We should always act in Sears best interests.

Gifts exchanged or offered are improper if the retail value exceeds $25. All gifts should be reported to your manager and any non-perishable gifts valued at over $25 should be returned with a note explaining the company's policy. Perishable gifts, such as food or candy, should be donated to a charitable organization or shared with other associates.

> **Q:** *What should I do if I am offered a gift and it would be embarrassing for me or for Sears to say no?*
>
> **A:** It depends on the nature and value of the gift. If it falls within the guidelines discussed above, accept it graciously. If it does not — if it is too valuable, or if it seems to require a "pay back" of some sort — then you must decline it.

Vehicles, appliances, other merchandise or the free use of any such item from an individual or organization that does business or seeks to do business with Sears are clearly improper. Free use of transportation provided by an individual or organization that does business, or seeks to do business, with Sears is clearly improper.

Examples of other permitted gifts and benefits include:

- Exchanging nominal gifts of the same approximate value between you and your personal friends at companies that do business with Sears;

- Giving and receiving promotional materials of nominal value such as pens or note pads;

- Accepting occasional entertainment, if it is business-related and approved by your manager. Good judgment should prevail.

Knowing where to draw the line when giving and receiving gifts requires common sense and good judgment. Avoid situations that may be subject to question or give the appearance of a conflict of interest.

Q: *Is it all right to seek a loan from a bank that does business with Sears?*

A: Yes, but you must not attempt to exploit the bank's relationship with Sears to get loan approval. The loan should be granted to you on the same basis as it would to any other customer.

Seminars and Meetings

We may attend a source-sponsored meeting, seminar, or event if there is a business reason and if our manager approves. Sears will pay for our transportation and lodging. We may accept host meals and entertainment connected with the event if offered to all participants.

Travel and Entertainment

All associates must travel in accordance with company policy and are encouraged to think like owners and minimize travel costs. We may not accept travel on source or vendor aircraft unless Sears reimburses the cost of our share of expenses.

Contests

If approved by a Sears manager, an associate may take part in legitimate contests sponsored and paid for by Sears or by sources. A legitimate contest is one which has clear criteria for winning and specific prizes, including merchandise or trips, awarded in accordance with rules. Sears must pay for any associates who attend contest-related activities in addition to contest winners.

Spouse Travel

Sears-reimbursed spouse travel should be limited to rare circumstances when strong social or business reasons require spouse attendance. An associate should obtain approval for such trips by management one level above that of his or her manager.

Q: *A computer software vendor has asked me to do some consulting work to help it improve its ability to sell products to Sears. I do not plan to charge for this help. May I provide this "free consulting" service to the vendor?*

A: No. Even though you do not receive payment for your work, you are privately using your knowledge of Sears to help a vendor, possibly to the detriment of both Sears and other competing vendors. However, you may respond to vendor surveys that are designed to improve service to Sears.

Q: *May I hire my son, who is grown and lives away from home, to plow the Sears parking lot if his rates are the best rates available?*

A: No. Regardless of how competitive the rates, if he is working under your supervision, this constitutes a conflict of interest.

Q: *My spouse is looking for part-time employment. My store is looking for help. May my spouse work in the same store as I do?*

A: Company policy allows members of the same family to work in the same unit, subject to manager approval, provided one does not have direct or indirect supervisory authority over the other and the two do not work in the same department at the same time.

Former Associates

Former associates working with vendors, consultants or other firms doing business with Sears must receive no special consideration. We must conduct business with former associates and their firms on an "arm's length" basis, just as we would with any other Sears vendor, consultant or business partner.

Family Members

The guidelines relating to personal investments, business dealings, political contributions, gift-giving and other payments described elsewhere in this booklet extend to family members residing with Sears associates. While we are not expected to monitor the business interests of all of our relatives, the members of our household should be familiar with these policies. Family involvement in an activity from which we are prohibited can result in a conflict of interest for us as serious as if we were involved directly.

Spouses and members of our household may hold a financial interest in, and may be employed by, businesses that offer products or services in competition with Sears. They also may be employed by organizations that do business with Sears, so long as this employment does not cause an actual or potential conflict of interest. A conflict of interest would occur, for example, if a family member were associated with a company whose business with Sears is completely or partially under your control or influence.

Associate Discount

Our Sears associate discount applies to merchandise and services purchased and paid for by ourselves, our spouses, and our dependent children who have a current discount identification card. We may not make purchases for later reimbursement by others not eligible for the discount. This includes parents and other ineligible family members.

Company Property and Records

Q: *Our store has clothing returned under the "Satisfaction Guaranteed" pledge. I am afraid it is going to be discarded. May I give it to a local charity?*

A: You may not do this on your own. Sears has policies for the return of merchandise that normally must be followed. While Sears often donates merchandise to worthwhile causes, you must consult your manager to obtain approval for any donation.

Q: *I have a strong suspicion that a fellow associate has stolen merchandise from the sales counter. How should I handle this?*

A: Do not accuse the associate directly. Report your concerns at once to your unit manager or Asset Protection Manager.

Q: *In my store, computer programs are used for customer demonstrations. As long as I use my own diskettes, may I make copies of the demonstration programs?*

A: No. The programs are used to help sales, but Sears does not own them or have the right to authorize copies. It is illegal for you to make personal copies of copyrighted computer software.

Associates may use company equipment, funds, supplies, facilities and other assets, as well as the services and labor of other Sears associates, only for legitimate business reasons on behalf of Sears. We may not take or use cash, merchandise or any other Sears property for personal purposes. Records must be kept accurately and confidential information must be protected at all times.

Company Assets

We all have a responsibility to care for all of the company's assets including merchandise, cash, supplies, facilities, the services of other Sears associates, and computer resources. If you see or suspect that another associate is stealing or otherwise not properly protecting company assets, you must report these concerns to your manager or to the Office of Ethics and Business Policy by calling 1-800-8ASSIST.

Sears funds may not be paid to others without a signed, written agreement or an approved, appropriately detailed invoice. We must never maintain or authorize the accumulation of company funds that are not recorded on Sears books and records. This includes the accumulation of such funds at Sears suppliers.

Q: *A not-for-profit organization for which I do volunteer work has asked me to coordinate this year's fundraising activities. May I write my appeal letter on Sears letterhead?*

A: No. Sears letterhead must be used only for official Sears business or for activities approved by Sears management.

Q: *As a Store General Manager, I sometimes receive calls from the local newspaper asking questions either about my store or about Sears in general. How should I respond?*

A: Respond as cooperatively as possible, but do not give out any confidential information such as data about the volume of sales, percentage increases or specific cost information.

Q: *I do volunteer work for a worthy organization that has recently asked me for a list of customers who have made major purchases at Sears so organization members can contact these people to solicit contributions. It's no trouble for me to get access to this list. May I share it?*

A: Records of Sears business transactions are confidential. Sharing them would violate both the privacy of our customers and company policy.

Using the Sears Name

The good name of Sears, Roebuck and Co. is the result of more than 100 years of hard work by our associates, superior service to our customers, and ethical dealings with our customers, our business partners and one another. To protect this asset, we must use the Sears name only for authorized company business and never in connection with personal or other activities unless we receive appropriate approval and an understanding that the use will be in accordance with Sears standards and values.

Company Records

Whenever we are asked to create or maintain reports or records, we are also responsible for the integrity of those records. We must not knowingly make any false or misleading entries in Sears books and records. All company financial reports, computer-based records, sales reports, expense accounts, time sheets and other similar documents must be completed accurately, completely and in accordance with Sears procedures and legal requirements governing the maintenance of records.

Confidential Information

Certain business information must be kept confidential, since disclosure could cause damage to Sears, our suppliers, customers and others. As a general rule, any matters not publicized by Sears should be viewed as confidential. We should never give confidential business information to people outside of Sears, or even to associates who have no need to know. Sears business relationships and financial, strategic, operational and promotional programs should be discussed with other associates only when necessary to perform our jobs.

All associates agree to preserve confidential information beyond our terms of employment with Sears.

Q: *May I release the addresses of the associates of our unit to an outside organization that wishes to offer them a merchandise discount?*

A: No. Regardless of the well-intentioned purpose, you may not release this confidential information to outsiders without the specific consent of the associate.

Q: *I forgot to file a change of medical plan status for my daughter, who was in college but recently dropped out. Last week she had some minor medical expenses. Is it all right to file one "final" claim if I change her status at the end of the school year?*

A: No. You are not entitled to that one "final" claim because she is no longer covered. Filing a claim now amounts to defrauding Sears. The right thing to do is to change her status immediately.

Q: *My father has asked to use my associate discount to purchase a refrigerator. Is this permissible?*

A: No, it is not permissible. The benefit is intended only for you and, under certain circumstances, for dependent members of your immediate household.

Associate Privacy

Records containing personal information about associates must be kept confidential. Access to such records is limited to managers and others with a specific need to use the information in the performance of their duties.

Apart from employment location, employment dates and job title, we should never provide any information about another Sears associate to anyone outside of the company without that associate's consent, unless the company is complying with a legal requirement such as a court order.

Company Benefits

We must always be truthful in providing information in connection with Sears benefit plans, including health, workers' compensation and associate discount plans. We may never obtain Sears benefits to which we are not entitled by providing inaccurate or incomplete information or by withholding information.

Complying with the Law

Sears associates must adhere strictly to all applicable laws and regulations in effect where the company does business. This requires adherence to both the letter and spirit of the law. Many of the policies expressed in this Code of Conduct are based on legal requirements.

Q: *I recently saw a good magazine article on selling strategy and showed it to my manager. She asked me to share the article with our team at an upcoming meeting. Is this all right?*

A: There is nothing wrong with your making a single working copy. But you should obtain permission or purchase reprints if you make copies for all team members.

Q: *I have just returned from a District sales meeting where I heard rumors about our excellent sales results that will be announced soon. I feel very proud of these results. May I share this information at an upcoming family gathering? I don't think anyone in the family has enough money to take advantage of this information.*

A: No. Even though members of your family may not be able to benefit directly from this non-public information, someone may pass it on to others who can. Passing on this non-public information is considered "tipping" and is prohibited.

Contract Negotiations

In negotiating contracts on behalf of Sears, we should deal fairly and honestly with all parties. We may not submit false or misleading documents or proposals.

Copyright Laws

We should never make unauthorized distribution of material from copyrighted books, magazines, newspapers, video tapes, or computer programs. While it may be all right to make a working copy for our own use, multiple copies made without permission are a violation of copyright laws.

Inside Information and Insider Trading

Our stock and other securities are traded publicly on major exchanges and the market prices of these securities are based upon what the public knows about Sears. Investors could gain an unfair advantage through inside, non-public information that could affect their decision to buy or sell securities. Trading on, or "tipping" others about material, non-public information about Sears, its subsidiaries, vendors or licensees threaten Sears integrity and may result in serious civil and criminal penalties for both individual associates and the company.

Many of us encounter inside information through the course of our normal business. Examples include news about our financial results prior to formal release, planned actions regarding our stock, important lawsuits, important contracts and senior management changes. The law forbids the purchase and sale of securities by anyone who has such material information which has not been made public through distribution over Dow Jones, other major news services, or through other publications widely distributed to the public.

Q: *What kind of securities are covered by the prohibition against insider trading?*

A: The prohibition applies to any securities, including common shares, preferred shares, bonds, debentures, put and call options and real estate limited partnership interests. A security need not be publicly traded on a stock exchange in order for it to be covered.

Although insider trading is a complex issue, we can avoid violations by being careful, exercising discretion and using common sense. As a general rule, we should never discuss inside information with family or friends, suggest they trade in Sears stock based on our inside information, or make personal investment decisions based on this information.

We should not speak with journalists, financial analysts or shareholders on behalf of Sears unless authorized to do so. We must use caution when asked to make speeches and even in casual social conversation.

Political Contributions and Activities

Associates may not give Sears funds, property, services or labor directly or indirectly, to any candidate, political organization or political party without specific approval of the Law department or Governmental Affairs department. This applies to any federal, state, or local election, or any referendum or to a lobbying effort at any level of government.

Bribery, Kickbacks and Foreign Business Dealings

We must never give Sears funds, property, services or labor, directly or indirectly, to any U.S. government official or agent, or foreign government official or agent in order to obtain business for Sears or to obtain any special or unusual treatment for the company.

Sears funds, property, services or labor must not be given, directly or indirectly, to anyone in an improper effort to obtain or retain business for Sears or any special or unusual treatment in connection with a business transaction.

Q: *May I make a personal contribution to a candidate for public office?*

A: Absolutely. The restrictions apply only to the use of Sears funds, property, services and labor.

Q: *If I give small payment to a customs official, I can bring back samples from my buying trips much more easily. The law calls these "facilitating" payments and allows them. Can I make these payments in order to make my job easier?*

A: No. Sears follows a higher standard. Payments to government officials or agents, no matter what their size or purpose, are not allowed.

Q: *My supervisor has asked me to use a solvent to clean up my sales area. The solvent has an unpleasant aroma. I often hear about unsafe chemicals. How can I find out whether this one is safe to use?*

A: In compliance with OSHA regulations, units maintain a Material Safety Data Sheet (MSDS) binder that describes potentially hazardous materials. If OSHA has designated this solvent as hazardous, measures to protect you will be discussed in the MSDS binder.

Q: *A number of cans of print cleaner are left over in our unit from when we had a printing operation. My supervisor has asked me to clean up this area. The cans appear to be rusting and I am concerned that they might leak. How should I dispose of the cans of print cleaner?*

A: Many materials such as these cans of print cleaner are classified as a hazardous substance and require special handling and disposal. You should not move these cans or drain them until you have contacted the Sears Environmental Group in the Facilities Planning department for guidance.

Workplace Safety

Sears places a high priority on providing all associates with a safe working environment. We must comply with all applicable Occupational Safety and Health Administration (OSHA) requirements and promptly correct any problems in the workplace that may jeopardize safety. Associates are responsible for bringing any problems or potential workplace safety violations they know about to their manager's attention.

Product Safety

Sears is committed to selling quality products that are safe for their intended uses, conform to all laws and regulations, and meet relevant industry safety standards. When Sears learns of a potential product safety problem, we cooperate with manufacturers and relevant government bodies to take appropriate action. Throughout the process, our principal goal is to ensure that consumers are adequately protected.

If you learn of a potential safety problem relating to Sears merchandise, you should report the problem to your unit manager immediately and contact the Sears Product Safety Office.

Environmental Protection

Sears is committed to improving the environment and preserving natural resources. This commits all of us to maintaining a high level of awareness on environmental matters, cooperating with government agencies, vendors and communities in environmental protection efforts and complying with all applicable environmental laws and regulations. It also requires the company and all associates to:

- Conserve resources through improving energy efficiency in our operations;
- Minimize the weight, volume, and toxicity of waste we generate; and
- Actively pursue opportunities to recycle.

IIA Research Foundation Board of Trustees 1996

IIA Research Foundation Board of Research Advisors 1996

Chairman
David S. Kowalczyk, CIA, CISA, *BlueCross BlueShield of Maryland*

Members
Charles H. "Bud" Allen, CBA, CISA, *PNC Bank Corporation*
Kevin M. Bannon, CPA, CFE, *Reebok International, Ltd.*
William M. Buhmann, *Bank Administration Institute*
William J. Duane Jr., CIA, CPA, CBA, *Rockchapel Associates, Inc.*
Gareth Evans, *England Intervention Board for Agricultural Produce*
John F. Garry, CIA, CPA, *Coopers & Lybrand L.L.P.*
David Hodgson, CPA, *Price Waterhouse LLP*
Dan R. Kelly, CPA, *Koch Industries, Inc.*
Kasey K. Kiplinger, CIA, *State of Iowa*
Amos Leviatov, CPA, *Israel Ministry of Finance*
Mary Lea McAnally, CIA, CA, *University of Texas at Austin*
Stephen W. Minder, CIA, CPA, CISA, CFE, *Archer Daniels Midland Company*
Glenda J. Minor, *Chrysler Corporation*
Jane F. Mutchler, PhD, CPA, *The Pennsylvania State University*
Claire Beth Nilsen, CBCO, *Outsourcing Partnership LLP*
Tage Rasmussen, *Aarhus School of Business*
Donald E. Ricketts, DBA, *University of Cincinnati*
Larry E. Rittenberg, PhD, CIA, CPA, *University of Wisconsin*
Robert S. Roussey, CPA, *University of Southern California*
Kathryn A. Schooley, CPA, *The Williams Companies*
Jay H. Stott, CIA, *Fidelity Investments*
Thomas J. Warga, CIA, MBA, *New York Life Insurance Company*
Joyce B. Williams, CFE, *Texas Guaranteed Student Loan*

IIA Staff Liaison
James H. Thompson, CIA, *Manager of Research*